CONTENTS

CONTENTS

ACKNOWLEDGEMENTS

I know that everyone who writes a book and begins to write the acknowledgements says there are just too many people to thank. And it's cliché but so very true. There really are too many people to thank. First and foremost, I need to give the hugest of thanks to every truck owner and chef who took the time out of his or her extremely busy schedule to sit down with me; they took the time out of their days and weeks to look through their recipes to find some to share. Going through this process, I realized just how little I knew about some of my favorite trucks. Getting to know all of the trucks and their proprietors more in-depth has been such a great experience for me. And while I appreciated all they did before I started this book, my appreciation has grown even more as I've gone through this process. Without all of them, there would have been no book for me to write. For them to open up their windows, doors and sometimes homes to Jim and me has been the most rewarding part of this process. I truly hope that this book does them all justice. I am blessed to call so many of them friends.

Having a flexible place to work for my "day job" has been such a blessing. Thank you to my employer, Floyd Shechter, and my co-workers for their support as I went through the process of writing this book during one of our busiest times. Having them bear with me as I took sometimes longer than normal lunches or came in a little after the office opened so I could meet with truck owners at breakfast has eased some of the stress, and I cannot thank them enough for that. And they were so understanding and supportive during those three unplanned days I took so that I could finish this manuscript—it's been a true blessing.

A project like this cannot be done without the support of friends and family—and there are so many of them that I could fill pages. I will find my own way to individually thank all of them. There are a few, though, whom I do feel need to be thanked here individually. Nothing happens without a mom and a dad. Thanks to my parents for bringing me to the land of opportunity. I try each and every day to make them proud

ACKNOWLEDGEMENTS

of me and to make sure that I do not squander the opportunities I am presented. Thanks to my aunt Donna and my cousin Kim—two of the most joyous people I have ever met. They both inspire me to be a better person. They have been confidantes when I needed them so desperately and have been there to provide me with a smile and an upbeat vibe when I've felt down and out. I appreciate them both more than they will ever know.

The photos in this book are all from a talented local photographer, Brooke Stephens. Thanks to Brooke for the time she spent heading to the trucks and the time she took to edit all of the pictures. I know the editing was no small task. Thank you for helping to bring my words to life through pictures.

There is one final thank-you that is perhaps the greatest of all: to Jim. He is the one who introduced me to food trucks. He is the one who has pushed me to try more "off the grid" foods. He is the true reason this book exists. If I had never met him, I have no idea how long it would have been before I ventured to the Grilled Cheeserie, or to any food truck for that matter. I know that without him, I would not have had the nerve to try a lot of the foods from the trucks. And that's a sad thought because I would have missed out on so much *fantastic* food. I know that it hasn't been easy living with me these last few months, as I've been stressed with my "day job" and writing this book.

Thank you, Jim, for sticking with me through this—you are the trooper of all troopers! And this book is truly my dedication to you.

INTRODUCTION

Growing up, I was a total midwestern girl. While I was born in Korea, I was adopted at just a few months old. I am just as much of a "corn-fed American" as those who are born in the United States. I grew up in Indiana, Minnesota and, finally, Alabama. With one parent working as a teacher and the other parent as a stay-at-home mom keeping four kids in line, I grew up on a lot of casseroles because Mom didn't have a lot of time to put together anything truly gourmet. I loved my mom's casseroles, even though, looking back, I realize they really weren't too flavorful. It's what you did to feed six people and survive on a single teacher's salary. Now, Mom, if you're reading this, you know I was always one of your best eaters so know that I loved your cooking. You always did the best with what you had available.

I would get in the way every night when my mom was cooking because I was fascinated by watching her. Plus, I always fancied being a cook when I grew up. Actually, I wanted to be a good cook because my grandma had told me that the way to a man's heart was through his stomach. And, well, I wanted a good man.

I moved to Nashville in 2002 for work. And it wasn't until sometime in 2011 that I started to notice friends mentioning going to a place called the Grilled Cheeserie. I thought to myself, "I love grilled cheese! I need to go to this place!" Unfortunately, when I looked it up, I couldn't ever find where the truck was headed or I wasn't familiar with the area of town it was in. I remember sitting at my computer while perusing social media pictures, thinking, "Wow, that's a really nice food truck." I started to follow the truck's movements almost like a stalker—but only an online stalker. It didn't really travel near my side of town during the day, so it was a bit difficult for me to try it out at lunchtime. Finally, on a cloudy Sunday morning in January 2012, my boyfriend, Jim (he pops up a lot in this book), looked at me and said, "You know. The Grilled Cheeserie is at Crema this morning for Sunday brunch." And I *finally* had my first food truck experience. I don't remember the name of the melt that I had, but I remember it had a fried egg on it. And thus began my romance with the food truck scene and culture here in Nashville.

It was about this time that a co-worker of mine mentioned that there was a weekly food truck lunch about three miles from my work. Since Jim lived only about a half mile away from the weekly location, we were able to meet for lunch. We would bring our tailgate chairs and a little foldout table. We would go through and split items from as many trucks as we could. As the crowd died down, we would walk back over and start chatting with the food truck owners. We began to build some friendships with many of the proprietors. It was also at this time that I would head back into the office all excited about what we had eaten or about a specific truck. I started telling my co-workers where they could find trucks near their homes over the weekend. I also started giving them tips on how to enjoy the best from the trucks. One of my co-workers mentioned that I should start a blog giving people the same tips I gave them. I thought about that and looked online; it turned out there really wasn't an active resource focused on the Nashville food truck scene at that time.

Needing a creative outlet and realizing that Nashville needed a good food truck resource—and also wanting to procrastinate a little bit at work—I did a little research on how to start a blog. Lo and behold, in May 2012, NashvilleFoodTruckJunkie.com was born. Since that time, I have become engrossed in food truck culture. While there are things that I will never fully understand, not being a food truck owner myself, I do know a lot more than the casual food truck patron. And I have made it my goal to share my experiences and what I've eaten and attempt to help people have the best possible experiences at the trucks.

What I hope to bring you in this book is a taste of some of the awesome trucks that are serving the streets of Nashville and middle Tennessee. Most of the trucks have been kind enough to share a recipe or two from the trucks or from their homes. I want to share some of the major events from the year where you can catch the trucks and also touch briefly on the history of food trucks in Nashville and the emergence of the Nashville Food Truck Association. There are new food trucks popping up all across the United States each week, and Nashville is no exception. And there are featured in this book some wise words shared with me by food truck owners that any new food truck owner should take to heart.

One of the things that draws me to the food trucks in general and to certain food trucks in particular is the personal connection I have with the owners. It is something that you rarely find in a brick-and-mortar restaurant but you can find in the food truck world—that personal connection to the people who create your food, the immediacy and the accessibility to the chef and the owner. It is one of the things that food truck owners rate high on their lists of favorite things about owning a food truck, and it is something that I want to share here. I am certainly going to talk about their food, but I also want to begin to create and share that personal connection that is unique to the food truck scene. I truly hope that comes through in the pages that follow.

THE SCENE

THE NASHVILLE FOOD TRUCK EXPLOSION AND THE NASHVILLE FOOD TRUCK ASSOCIATION

The Nashville food truck scene has been around for a lot longer than most people realize, and the roadside taquerías have been around for much longer than that. Most truck owners will agree that the first of the gourmet-style food trucks was, coincidentally enough, a taco truck: Mas Tacos Por Favor, which started back in 2008. There were a few other food trucks to hit the scene shortly after Mas Tacos paved the way. Of those original trucks, only Mas Tacos is still operational, now running a brick-and-mortar location in East Nashville.

By 2010–11, the food truck explosion had already taken place in many cities around the country: Portland, Los Angeles, New York and Chicago. Television shows were popping up featuring food trucks, and Nashville was finally starting to attract a few ambitious individuals who wanted to start them up. The Grilled Cheeserie was followed by a small group of trucks that included Riffs Fine Street Food, Hoss' Loaded Burgers, Smoke Et Al, Moovers and Shakers, Deg Thai, Jonbalaya and Yayo's OMG, among some of the more recognizable names.

In 2011, food trucks were so new to the Nashville area that the food truck owners had no real resource explaining the regulations, code requirements and other legalese that was necessary for a food truck to open and operate. It was very much an idea of go ahead and try it, then ask for forgiveness from Metro Nashville after the fact if there was, indeed, an issue. To clarify, no one was breaking any laws because, at the time, there really was nothing written down. While now there are set zones downtown where the food trucks can park, there were no such regulations in 2011. As trucks such as the Grilled Cheeserie started to amass large crowds wherever they went, Metro Nashville began to take notice, as did the Hospitality and Tourism Association.

After seeing the hurdles that other cities have faced, Nashville's food truck owners came together as a single unit to work with Metro Nashville to find the best situation for the city, the food trucks and the Hospitality and Tourism Association. With guidance from a gentleman named Dennis Alpert, the food truck owners created the Nashville Food Truck Association (NFTA).

The NFTA has a mission statement that, at its most basic core, says it is a group of food truck owners who come together as a unified voice that works with local legislators to bring the best of the small business food truck owner to the streets and residents of middle Tennessee. It also strives to ensure that the trucks in the NFTA are focused on doing things the right way, both legislatively and from a culinary perspective. It wants to ensure that the food truck community always has its best foot forward. You can visit the official NFTA website to read its full mission statement: www.nashvillefoodtruckassociation.com.

Yayo's OMG owner Chef Yayo says, "I believe that the NFTA must focus on staying united and strong as a group of small business owners so we can properly support our growing food truck scene."

Every food truck that operates affects the food truck community. And it is important to note that not every truck you see operating is a member of the NFTA. Yet the reputation of the trucks in the NFTA is affected by experiences the casual consumer has at trucks that are not in the association. Trucks that are members of the NFTA will have stickers prominently displayed somewhere on the vehicles or in their service windows. I also have a list of current members as of the date of this writing. In my talks with food truck owners in the last few months, I've stated the following several times, and they all completely agree with me: If a restaurant puts out a poor product or has bad service to the casual consumer, it is bad only for that restaurant. That consumer will have no problem going to a different restaurant the very next day. But when it comes to food trucks, if casual consumers receive poor service or bad food, or they feel prices are too high, that experience will affect their next experience at a food truck, if they even have one. So it is important for the NFTA to focus on standards of service and food put out the windows of its member trucks. The NFTA does require that its members have a ninety or higher health rating. Most trucks have that beautiful yellow health inspection sheet proudly displaying one hundred. I say beautiful because it is something to be proud of. How many restaurants have you been to that have a one hundred health inspection rating? If you think that food trucks are roach coaches, think again!

Two Guys In A Lunchbox's Jeremy Rakestraw comments, "It is a privilege to be a member and to uphold the high standards and promote a positive working partnership with others in our industry."

THE SCENE

Being a member of the association is not a truck's guaranteed stamped ticket to longevity or popularity in the Nashville street food scene. First and foremost, one needs to know and understand that and take it to heart. Providing the eaters of Nashville with outstanding service and ridiculously delicious food is what will cement a truck's place in the street food scene. What being a member of the association will do for a truck is make it a part of an organized community of food trucks. There is also the added benefit of being part of a group of food truck owners working and having a relationship with the legislators of Metro Nashville. By having a relationship with legislators, I mean that the association knows whom to contact at Metro Codes, the Health Department or the Hospitality and Tourism Association in order to discuss any issues that need to be worked through. If you were on your own, would you know where to begin the process of the who, how, what and where to ask your questions?

One of the other benefits of the association is being part of a group of people who all know exactly how a new owner feels, who have all experienced the exact same things and can help new members work through the issues, the questions and perhaps even the hard times. The NFTA is a resource meant to help owners develop better trucks and better businesses. It can help trucks find new locations or get them set up and scheduled at established locations. The association also organizes some of the major food truck events throughout the year, and being a member means having one foot in the door at these events.

As with any business decision, it's important to do your research before jumping in. The association is not without its challenges. It is a young organization, so it needs to get through those "terrible twos" and oh-so-difficult teen years that every organization faces before it finally hits its stride. I am not a member of the NFTA, as I am not a food truck owner, so I am not at the meetings and am not privy to the little ins and outs that go on there. While I see certain challenges from a consumer's standpoint, the actual challenges that the NFTA faces might be different from what a consumer would understand about the food truck business. It's not my place to list any specific challenges, but I do know that every organization, whether it is in its infancy or has reached maturity, is faced with challenges and drawbacks. While there are a plethora of benefits of being a member of the NFTA, any potential new member should always make sure that the vision, mission and current direction of the organization ties in with his or her own vision, mission and direction. The best way to do that is to speak with as many members of the association as possible.

For more information on the Nashville Food Truck Association, you can e-mail general inquiries to nftainfo@gmail.com, or go online to its website (www.nashvillefoodtruckassociation.com) and check out the section entitled "Join NFTA."

Current members as of March 2014 (in alphabetical order) include Armory Eats, Bacon Nation, Biscuit Love Truck, Blue Monkey Shaved Ice, Bradley's Curbside Creamery, Confeastador, Crankee's Pizza, Crepe A Diem, Cupcake Collection,

DegThai, Delta Bound, Doughworks, the Grilled Cheeserie, Hip Sweet Subs, Hoss' Loaded Burgers, Itty Bitty Donuts, Jeni's Splendid Ice Cream, Jonbalaya, Julia's Bakery, the Mobile Chef, Moovers and Shakers, Music City Pie Co., Pappy's Mobile Café, Patty Wagon, Pita Pit, Retro Sno, Riffs Fine Street Food, the Rolling Feast, Rollin Smoke, Smoke Et Al, Smokin' Thighs, Smoothie King, Sum Yum Yum, Tiger Meat, Two Guys In A Lunchbox, Waffle Boss and Yayo's OMG.

THE BIG FOOD TRUCK EVENTS

While during the week, the trucks are located at numerous locations and business parks throughout middle Tennessee, there are a few places and events throughout the year where you can find a plethora of trucks all in one place.

On a smaller scale, several of the farmers' markets around town—from Franklin to 12 South to Donelson (and sometimes the Nashville Farmers' Market)—will have at least one or two trucks, if not a few more depending on the size. The local breweries that operate taprooms also have developed relationships with food trucks. Operating a taproom means the brewery must offer food, but most breweries have a singular focus: beer. So to pair up and have a food truck on-site is a win-win for both parties. The breweries can focus on the beer, and the food trucks can focus on the food. Yazoo Taproom bar manager Alan Fey says:

> We love the variety of options for food out there. But it's also great because it's another local member of the community. And they can park out front, and we can tell people, "Hey, so and so food truck is here." We don't want to be a restaurant. We want to be a place where people get can get great beer. So if we can have someone here who handles the food side of things, it makes our lives easier, and it makes things more interesting for our customers, too.

Tennessee Brew Works, Black Abbey Brewing, Jackalope Brewery and Corsair Artisan Distillery and Taproom are just a few of the other local taprooms where you can also find trucks on a regular basis.

In 2012, the NFTA held its inaugural Nashville Street Food Awards. Held in conjunction with Musician's Corner (a free concert series in the spring and fall), the event brought together nearly every food truck in Centennial Park. The trucks ran a normal service throughout the day but also were able to enter a variety of categories ranging from Best Drink and Best Taco to Best Deep Fried and Best Dessert. There were nine different categories. Very similar to a barbecue competition, the trucks were given containers in which to place their entries. There were specific turn-in times for

each category. The entries were then judged blindly by a group of six judges. The scores were based on presentation, taste and overall experience.

I was lucky to be asked to be a judge of three categories in this competition and also three categories for the Second Annual Nashville Street Food Awards held in 2013. The biggest perk of being a judge was that many of the trucks entered items they do not serve on their trucks. They are items created specifically for the competition. After judging my three assigned categories, I later discovered what the food truck owners had entered. And I was shocked (in a good way) by some of the entries. Sometimes it was because I didn't realize a truck was so versatile. Other times, it was because the truck went out of the box to create the entry.

While it was advertised that the trucks would have small bites available (in addition to the normal-sized entrees) so that patrons could try as many trucks as possible, this didn't always happen. One should always be prepared for full-sized portions—bring friends and split dishes; then you can try more! Delta Bound did have a small bites menu at the 2013 Nashville Street Food Awards and was one of the most popular trucks, selling out in just about two or three hours. I hope that at the 2014 Nashville Street Food Awards, more trucks will add the small bites. This is a prime event for exposure. But if a truck is offering only its normal serving size, most people will be able to eat from only one or two trucks before they are sated and ready to just sit and enjoy the free live music. Give them a bite, and give them the opportunity to come back for a full order.

Speaking of Musician's Corner, this is a free concert series that runs during the spring and early summer and then again in the fall. This event happens every Saturday starting about noon and running through the early evening. There is a lineup of several performers throughout the day. Local brewery Yazoo hosts a beer garden for those twenty-one and over. And there are at least three or four food trucks on a rotating basis.

WISE WORDS FOR PROSPECTIVE FOOD TRUCK OWNERS

In the process of doing this book, I not only wanted to give a behind-the-scenes look at the trucks, their owners and the food, but I also wanted to get some tips from current truck owners that might be helpful to anyone out there who is considering a life in food truck ownership.

Biscuit Love Truck's Karl Worley and Sarah Worley advise, "Concept really defines you. Know your concept. If you look at the trucks that have been successful and have had longevity in this market, they have a defined concept. Know what you do, and do *that* well. You cannot do a little bit of everything and do a little bit of everything well."

Delta Bound's Jessica Mobley adds, "Concept has to be solid and it has to be relevant."

Concept, concept, concept. Truck owner after truck owner after truck owner reiterated the importance of concept. Even if the menu changes, when people look at a truck, from the wrap to the logo to the slogan (if it has one), they need to know exactly what to expect. If they look at a truck and really have no clue what kind of food it serves, there is a good chance that the truck will be passed over without even a perusal of the menu. The concept also needs to be relevant to the consumer; a truck owner needs to understand *who* his or her consumer is when creating a concept. While it would be nice to think the consumer is everyone in Nashville, that's not the case. But it's important to make sure that the concept appeals to enough people to make the business successful.

The Confeastador's Christian Rodricks suggests, "Befriend everybody."

Bare Naked Bagel's Robert Kane reflects, "I was shocked at how open everyone has been. When we went to meet Amy and Jonathan [Loco Donuts], the information and advice they gave us in that first meeting really drove us to buy the truck. It's been really nice to see the amount of people who reach out to us and vice versa. Just how open and willing to give advice everyone is."

The food truck community is just that—a community. And honestly, in talking with food truck owners, it has become clear that it's a very tightknit community, one that helps those in need. One that pushes its fellow trucks to do better and be better. There will come a time when everyone has a flat tire, as happened to the Confeastador on one occasion. The Confeastador's owners were able to ask their fellow food truck proprietors where to find the right tire at the right price point at a place conveniently located near to where they were. Within moments, they were bombarded with recommendations.

In my day job, I coordinate food trucks at one of the properties once a week. Due to the weather, one truck had to delay some truck repairs by one day, which caused it to miss its scheduling at our property. I asked the owner if he knew of anyone who could take his spot, and within moments, he e-mailed me back with a replacement truck. There is always a truck willing to help out another truck. We have even seen cases where food truck owners help out fellow food trucks in their kitchens for special events. And we have heard stories from one food truck owner about how, on her second day of business, a fellow food truck owner (on his day off) saw that she was in a bit of a pickle with a long line and offered to hop on board and help her out (which he did). This community of food truck owners is accepting and always willing to help out a friend in need.

Nick Moeller of Doughworks notes, "You need to learn how to weed out the bad events from the good. Do your research on a request before accepting."

In a truck's first year, it's going to struggle to get in the rotation at several of the corporate properties that have regulars on set days. And new owners might start to feel like they just need to accept whatever invitation comes their way, but not everything will be worth their time or money. Nick Moeller tells a story about being invited to a flea market. It was during his first year, and any invitation was graciously appreciated. Upon arrival, it became apparent that the flea market was in the middle of nowhere, and there were only two other vendors there. Nick said that not a single patron made his or her way to this middle-of-nowhere flea market. The gas it took to drive the truck for an hour-long trip, the wear and tear on the generator and the cost of labor during the event, as well as the cost of labor prepping for the day—it was all to sell *one* doughnut. It was a lesson learned. And it is a lesson that Moeller would like to help novice food truck owners avoid learning the hard way.

Talk with other food truck owners to learn the questions that should be asked of event organizers in order to weed out the good events from the bad events. It's true that in the first year, it's important to get a truck's name and brand out there, but that doesn't mean it needs to serve at events where it likely won't break even. Food truck owners are in control of which events they attend. Early in a truck owner's career, it can be exciting to simply be invited, but don't let someone try to manipulate the popularity of food trucks by using your truck to draw people to their event. You will end up losing more than the event coordinator. Every business owner needs to make the right decisions for his or her business. And accepting every event invitation received is not a good business decision.

Retro Sno's Elizabeth Nunnally advises, "You get what you pay for. Investing more in your equipment allows you to focus on the business instead of having to focus on fixing things."

Yayo's OMG's Yayo Jimenez notes, "The truck is the base of the business. If it doesn't move, you don't move. So definitely it is an extremely important factor."

Sum Yum Yum's Kong and Tricia warn, "Beware of where you purchase your food truck."

For a truck that shuts down during the winter, having mechanical problems during the spring and summer can be devastating. And that is just what happened to Retro Sno in 2013. Due to severe truck issues, it was forced to shut down in July instead of November. As Retro Sno co-owner Elizabeth Nunnally notes, it is better to make sure you are purchasing good-quality equipment instead of buying the cheapest equipment. As a start-up food truck, this is the pitfall into which many new owners fall. They say, "I bought what I could afford." It's a smart decision to really take the time to research what you are buying. Don't jump into the driver's seat because you think something is all you can get. Look at your budget and your business plan, and make sure you can invest the right amount into the equipment. This is your business. If your truck can't run, your business can't run. If your oven doesn't work, your business can't go to work. And I've heard many horror stories of scam artists selling food trucks to unsuspecting newbies. Be vigilant. Do your research. Invest in your equipment.

Nunnally, of Retro Sno, adds, "One thing I'm glad we did was we spent months on the branding and getting that right before we launched. Branding is just so important. And we were so busy after we launched that we never would have had time to develop that properly if we had waited."

Going back to concept, but from a different perspective, building a business is really about building a brand. Many new owners think, "I'm a food truck, and my food will do all the talking." But in order for the food to do the talking, people have to come to the truck. And that doesn't happen without a brand. It's tempting to just get the truck up and running as quickly as possible, but that is exactly what you shouldn't do. In talking to food truck owners, many of them took months developing their business plans. It wasn't on a Saturday that they thought of the idea and on Monday that they bought a truck and one month later they were on the roads. They spent a fair amount of time on the front end to develop the concept and brand. Then they spent several months or sometimes years preparing the truck before they were able to serve food. You can't show up in a plain truck and expect people to walk up and order. Customers don't want to eat from a truck they feel is a rush job. A brand is a representative of how the truck prepares its food and the quality it brings to the table. If an owner doesn't care about his brand, consumers will ask, "How much does he care about the food?" Take the time and do it right before opening.

Nunnally continues, "Resilience is huge. You have to be able to adapt and bounce back."

Hoss' Loaded Burgers' Dallas Shaw adds, "You obviously don't want to build in scenarios where you go out of business, but you need to make sure you know how to survive under a worst-case scenario."

The stats on small businesses that close each year, especially in the food service industry, are pretty astounding. The stats on food trucks that close, and those that close in the first year, are even more astounding. There are a few reasons for this. First, it is crucial to be able to bounce back and adapt in times of adversity. It would have been easy for Retro Sno to decide to close its window after its 2013 truck problems. In fact, that's when most trucks *do* close. It's a double cost: you can't make any money because your truck is out of commission, and on top of that, you have the cost of fixing the truck. When these truck issues last from days, then turn into weeks and then, unfortunately, months, it can get expensive, and unless you have some resiliency to work through that downtime, you won't be able to reopen your window.

So when you are developing your business plan, conceive of a worst-case scenario. Resiliency is a lot easier to possess when you have a plan to follow. And being able to adapt is critical. Jay Jenratha, with DegThai, bought his truck with everything already set up inside, so he wasn't able to build in the appropriate equipment to have a wok on the truck. This is something he would love to have, not only to save time preparing food on the truck, but also so he can prepare a more versatile menu. But he has adapted his menu and continues to grow his brand and his truck, despite not having a wok. Both Retro Sno and DegThai are on most people's lists of the top-ten food trucks in Nashville. These are two prime examples of resiliency and adaptation, living proof that they are a *must* for any food truck owner.

These are just a few of the tips and thoughts from some of our successful Nashville food truck owners—some things to keep in mind if you are thinking about starting a food truck. It's clear that the first rule is don't rush into purchasing a truck. My first suggestion would be to talk to current food truck owners, not just at the truck, but also schedule time with them over coffee or a meal. Talk thoroughly with them. And talk to a lot of them. Be honest, and make sure you are able to take constructive criticism. And be sure to contact me before you open so we can meet and I can get excited about your truck and start helping you build a buzz as your opening nears!

BISCUIT LOVE

Biscuit Love is truly a love story between its owners, Karl and Sarah Worley. And Nashville gets to be the beneficiary of that love in each and every biscuit the Worleys make and we eat.

The story goes that when Karl and Sarah met, Sarah told him, basically, that the relationship couldn't go anywhere because she was heading to culinary school. Karl replied, "What if I went with you?" But there's more to the story than that.

I asked Sarah when it was that she fell in love with food. Sarah said it began when she went to a restaurant called Zola, which was run by one of Nashville's most well-respected female chefs, Deb Paquette. The meal Sarah enjoyed there was "one of the most amazing meals" she had ever had eaten. Finding out that Zola had a female chef opened Sarah's eyes to the possibility of the culinary arts. After a brief visit to Europe, where Sarah fell in love with the culture of food and family, and thinking back to that meal at Zola, Sarah decided on a life change. She enrolled in Johnson & Wales culinary school. Enter Karl.

From his grandmother's biscuits and potatoes to his grandfather's apple butter, Karl has loved food for as long as he can remember. After getting the heck out of dodge (aka Bristol), he discovered that girls loved guys who could cook and cook well. So he started really honing his love of cooking and food. After taking a few courses at Nashville State Community College's culinary school, Karl went and knocked on the back door at a restaurant called Zola (sound familiar?). Deb Paquette answered the door. Let's just say that after an on-the-spot tryout, Karl thought that the culinary arts were not in his future. Enter Sarah.

The rest is history, and what a history these last two years have been. Biscuit Love officially opened its windows in the late winter/early spring of 2012. Since that time,

it has been featured on *The Today Show* and the Cooking Channel's *Unique Eats* and *Eat Street*, and it was recently a feature at one of the largest and most prestigious food festivals in North America: the South Beach Food & Wine Festival in Miami in February 2014. And I can't think of two more deserving people than Karl and Sarah.

You now know the story, but what about the food, right? Going back to Karl's salad days, biscuits were fond memories from what he calls his "redneck childhood." And biscuits are something that Karl makes well. He utilizes a philosophy of doing as much from scratch as possible and as much from locally sourced foods as possible. He knows the farmer who grows the grain for his flour and the millers who mill his flour. And it travels less than three hundred food miles to get to Karl's truck. He has developed these relationships so that he knows how the ingredients he puts into his biscuit sandwiches are created. Having so much locally sourced and unprocessed materials are what really help make Biscuit Love one of the trucks that stand out from the pack.

I can vividly remember my first visit to the Biscuit Love truck. It was at the Nashville Farmers' Market, and Karl and Sarah were not yet in the Airstream trailer they have now. We (Jim and myself) walked up to their truck, and Sarah greeted me with a hug. Jim is a Nashville Hot

Chicken fanatic, so he was looking forward to their Princess Biscuit, which is a biscuit with a piece of hot chicken on it. I was looking forward to trying the Gertie (an ode to their daughter), which is a biscuit smothered in caramelized banana jam, homemade peanut butter and Olive & Sinclair chocolate gravy. Thanks to Elvis, the South has a very strong relationship with the banana, peanut butter and chocolate combination. Needless to say, the Gertie is one of Biscuit Love's most popular items and is a mainstay on its menu.

The Princess Biscuit is another mainstay. Let me go into a little more detail about the Princess Biscuit. Karl perfectly fries a dark meat piece of chicken, and it is then tossed in his hot chicken sauce. Cutting open the biscuit, he places the hot chicken on the biscuit. He then tops that with homemade pickles and mustard and then drizzles some local honey on it before topping it with the top half of the biscuit. It's a monster of a biscuit sandwich.

Another mainstay menu item is the East Nasty, which is a biscuit sandwich with a piece of buttermilk-fried chicken and local cheddar cheese covered in local homemade sausage gravy. Again, this is a beast of a biscuit sandwich. Most people have to eat this with a fork and knife. There is a trick to eating both this and the Princess as sandwiches instead of with utensils. And if you ever see me out and about, I will be more than happy to show you how it's done!

While New York might have the Cronut, Nashville now has the Bonut, thanks to Biscuit Love. Karl says that one time, as he was making biscuits, he had leftover pieces and didn't want to waste them. So he thought up the Bonut, taking these smaller pieces and deep-frying them. Most of the time, they are filled with a mascarpone fruit

curd and then rolled in sugar and topped with a homemade fruit preserve. They are every child's dream and every adult's guilty pleasure.

You don't realize how versatile a biscuit can be until you visit the Biscuit Love truck. From the John T., a fried catfish biscuit, to truly gourmet versions of a sloppy Joe and a burger, the biscuit serves as a lot more than just a vessel for a breakfast sandwich. Karl and Sarah are also starting to build in a few specialty items that are more than just biscuits, from Karl's interpretation of ramen with his Redneck Ramen to their newest menu item, the Lindstrom, which is a shaved Brussels sprout salad tossed with a fresh and lively lemon vinaigrette and toasted hazelnuts and topped with a poached egg. No biscuit is harmed in the making of the Lindstrom. It is fresh. It is light. It is healthy. And it is delicious!

I had the opportunity recently to sit down with Karl and Sarah. I asked them if they could go back in time, what would they tell themselves that might have made their journey a little smoother. They both replied that they wouldn't tell themselves a thing. Sarah then added, "Actually, I would tell ourselves to buckle up, and it would be worth *every* struggle. Because this has been the freakin' ride of our lives."

What does the future hold for Karl and Sarah Worley and the Biscuit Love truck? Karl smirks and says he still has a few more food truck concepts in his back pocket. Both Karl and Sarah agree that when the time is right, they could see a transition of Biscuit Love from truck to brick and mortar. This is a common goal for most food trucks.

Biscuit Love is truly Nashville's quintessential "brunch truck." You can find Karl and Sarah each Saturday morning at the Franklin Farmers' Market located at The Factory in Franklin, Tennessee, and each Sunday for brunch at White's Mercantile located in the 12 South District of Nashville, Tennessee. They are available for catering, and you can check their website (www.biscuitlovetruck.com), Facebook page and Twitter feed (@BiscuitLuvTruck) for any other pop-up locations.

Biscuit Love's Banana Jam
(Recipe provided by Karl and Sarah Worley)

2 cups granulated sugar
¼ cup water
3 cups bananas, sliced
½ teaspoon salt
1 tablespoon lime juice
1 tablespoon vanilla extract
Warm biscuits

Mix the sugar and ¼ cup water in a heavy-bottomed large saucepan on high heat until the mixture caramelizes. The water will need to evaporate before the sugar will caramelize. Once the caramel reaches a deep brown color, turn the heat to low and carefully add the bananas. Stir with a wooden or heat-resistant spoon until the bananas begin to break, which should be 10 to 15 minutes. Add the salt, lime juice and vanilla and remove from the heat. Serve over warm biscuits.

Biscuit Love's Family Reserve Biscuits
(Recipe provided by Karl and Sarah Worley)

2 cups flour, low-protein, all-purpose
3 tablespoons granulated sugar
2 teaspoon baking powder
1 teaspoon kosher salt
2 tablespoon very cold butter
2 tablespoon very cold lard
1²/₃ cup buttermilk, full fat
*Chef's note: If using self-rising flour, omit the baking powder

For shaping:
1½ cups flour, low-protein, all-purpose
4 tablespoons butter, melted

Preheat oven to 425 degrees. Butter the bottom and sides of a 10-inch cast-iron skillet. Mix together dry ingredients. Grate the butter and lard into the dry mixture and cut into dry ingredients. Pour buttermilk into mixture and stir until just combined. It should resemble cottage cheese.

Using a 4-ounce scoop or spoon, place a dollop of dough into a bowl with the remaining flour. Sprinkle flour on top. Pick up the dough ball and gently shake off excess flour. Repeat. Place balls into skillet very close together. Bake for 20 minutes, until golden brown and set. Pour butter over biscuits as soon as they are out of the oven.

Bradley's Curbside Creamery

In the process of meeting with Nashville-area food truck owners, owner Bradley Freeman and his mom, Lynne, invited us into their commissary to help make some ice cream while we got our questions answered. The catch? We had to come prepared with a flavor idea. We had chosen to make what is now known at Bradley's Curbside Creamery as Cheesecake Junkie. It is chocolate ice cream with chunks of cheesecake and a raspberry swirl. I'm pretty happy to report that it is very tasty!

Bradley's Curbside Creamery actually came on the scene as Hit and Miss Ice Cream back in 2010 and was focused on a lot of carnivals, fairs and big events. The original truck looked like a mini wooden barn that was actually a mobile trailer and not a truck. At the time, Lynne was attending her fair share of craft fairs and events with her embroidery business. At event after event, both Bradley and Lynne would see that there was not something there drawing a lot of patrons. After one particular event, Lynne noticed there was an ice cream vendor who was also making cobblers, and it was doing very well. She came home and mentioned the idea to Bradley, who started to do extensive research on making homemade ice cream. A visit to the Williamson County Fair brought them to a gentleman who was actually looking to sell his ice cream business and enter retirement. And thus begins the story of Bradley's Curbside Creamery. After developing some initial flavors, Hit and Miss Ice Cream hit the event circuit. Hit and Miss Ice Cream was named after the 1928 John Deere Hit and Miss motor that was originally in use to make the ice cream when they started.

By 2012, the food truck scene in Nashville had started to find its stride, and Hit and Miss was starting to transition from the fair circuit to street food truck events and locations. Along with that transition, Bradley and Lynne bought a traditional street food truck and rebranded the business to Bradley's Curbside Creamery, which causes less confusion over who they are. They still utilize the mobile trailer as Hit and Miss for carnivals, fairs and some of their larger events. It is now a backup so they can be at more than one place at the same time. The baby blue Bradley's Curbside Creamery truck is hard to miss, and Bradley and Lynne are looking to update the truck with new graphics and perhaps a new wrap to add to the experience of visiting the truck.

The more I visit Bradley's Curbside Creamery, the more I realize that it serves some of the best ice cream in the entire city of Nashville. Having been inside Bradley and Lynne's commissary and having helped to actually make a flavor, I can appreciate the work that goes into each batch of ice cream. If Bradley is going full speed, he can make roughly one hundred gallons of ice cream in a single day. And there are weeks and months during the summer fair season when he has to do just that in order to keep up with demand.

Now, even though I helped to create the Cheesecake Junkie flavor, I have to admit that when it comes to my favorite mainstay flavor at Bradley's, it has to be Cookies and Cream. The mix Bradley and Lynne use to make their ice cream is high quality. You can literally taste the cream in Cookies and Cream. And who doesn't love Oreo cookie pieces in ice cream? Bradley's favorite ice cream is the Orange Dreamsicle, which to me tastes exactly like those orange push pops I remember so fondly from my childhood. For a White Trash experience (it's the name of the float), Bradley adds a scoop of Orange Dreamsicle to a cup of Mountain Dew. The citrus from the Mountain Dew complements the ice cream, and the Orange Dreamsicle brings out the best of the Mountain Dew. It's the best White Trash experience you will ever have. In case you are wondering about the name White Trash, it was inspired by an episode of the TV show *My Name Is Earl* in which one character shouts to another to see if he got the Mountain Dew for the babies' bottles.

I'm not typically a fan of mocha-flavored ice creams, but I have to say that Bradley's Curbside Creamery's mocha ice cream was a pleasant surprise. Jim and I have discovered that the mocha ice cream makes for a good beer float when mixed with a high-end craft chocolate milk stout. I was sitting down with a few other food truck owners, and more than one of them mentioned that Bradley's Peanut Butter ice cream is their hands-down favorite. I went to try it one Saturday, and wouldn't you know, Bradley's was sold out! Luckily, I organized to have Bradley's visit one of the properties that my day job company manages, and I was happy to discover that Peanut Butter was in stock. After a small taste, I immediately understood why it was a favorite of so many food truck owners. It was the perfect mix of peanut butter and cream. I felt like I was eating some of the best peanut butter ever, and it was even better because it wasn't sticking to the roof of my mouth.

While Cookies and Cream is my favorite mainstay flavor, the seasonal flavor Crème de Menthe is probably my ultimate favorite. Maybe it's because it is available for only a limited time each year, or maybe it's the chunks of Girl Scout Thin Mint cookies, but it is far and away the most phenomenal ice cream out there.

From Sugar Free Butter Pecan to Banana to the standards Vanilla and Chocolate, you are bound to find a flavor at the truck that you will love and just have to take home. I typically end up getting a waffle cone, especially when Lynne is making them fresh on the truck. The smell of waffles wafting off the truck is just as enticing as freshly popped popcorn at the movie theater.

One of the cool things I'd like to mention is that Bradley's Curbside Creamery won Best Drink at the Nashville Street Food Awards in back-to-back years. In the inaugural year, 2012, it won with one of its ice cream floats. And this past year, 2013, it won the category with a Mexican hot cocoa with homemade marshmallows. So if you are a shake, float or malt fan, Bradley's definitely has some drink-making chops to go along with its ice cream–making skills. At the most recent 2013 Nashville Street Food Awards, Bradley's also walked away with third place in the Best Olive & Sinclair category for its profiteroles, stuffed with its Peanut Butter ice cream and drizzled with Olive & Sinclair chocolate sauce. It also tied for third place in the Best of the Best (Overall).

I've said it on social media and to people I encounter, and I'll say it here: Bradley's Curbside Creamery is serving up ice cream that rivals any major ice cream conglomerate. Try one of its ice cream pies. Get a waffle cone. Try a float or a shake or, if you ask nicely, a malt. My freezer stays full of Bradley's Curbside Creamery treats, and I do not see that changing anytime soon.

Bradley's Curbside Creamery is available for any event, from birthday parties to weddings to corporate events to property management fire drills. To get in touch with Bradley and Lynne, find Bradley's Curbside Creamery on Facebook, Twitter feed (@bradleystruck) and their website (www.bradleyscurbsidecreamery.com).

Bradley's Curbside Creamery's Homemade Hot Fudge Sauce
(Recipe provided by Lynne Freeman)

^{2}/₃ cup heavy cream
½ cup light corn syrup
¹/₃ cup brown sugar
¼ cup unsweetened cocoa powder
¼ teaspoon salt
6 ounces bittersweet chocolate, chopped (split into 2 servings of 3 ounces each)
2 tablespoons unsalted butter
1 teaspoon vanilla extract

In a medium saucepan over medium heat, combine heavy cream, corn syrup, brown sugar, unsweetened cocoa powder, salt and 3 ounces of the chopped bittersweet chocolate. Bring mixture to a low boil, stirring frequently until the chocolate is completely melted.

Reduce heat to medium-low and continue to stir. Cool for an additional 3 to 5 minutes.

Remove from heat. Add the remaining 3 ounces of chopped bittersweet chocolate, along with the butter and vanilla. Stir until sauce is smooth. Cool slightly before using or transferring to a storage container. Store chilled. Re-warm in a saucepan or microwave prior to serving.

Confeastador

Growing up, chef Christian Rodrick's first foray into cooking was making grilled cheese sandwiches for himself and his brother after school. He then elevated that to making even better grilled cheese sandwiches. After spending time as a bike messenger, Christian decided he'd had enough of getting hit by cars and really started to get serious about cooking. After attending culinary school and working in several fine-dining establishments, Christian and his longtime friend Travis moved to Nashville with the goal of starting up their very own food truck.

Feeling that Nashville was an up-and-coming food destination, Christian and Travis also fell in love with the feel of the city and its beautiful landscape. While the Confeastador truck is new to the people of Nashville, having opened its windows in late 2013, the truck has been in the works for about three years now. "Truck issues"—something every food truck owner can relate to—was the reason behind their delay. Travis jokes that they feel like they are general contractors, having done so much plumbing, tiling, flooring and mechanical work on the truck. In fact, when I asked them the question, "If you could go back in time and give yourselves advice knowing what you know now, what would you tell yourselves?" both of their answers related to the truck. Christian joked that he would buy a better truck. Travis added that he would make sure they had a good mechanic go with them when they looked at the truck to make sure they knew ahead of time what issues they might face.

Luckily, after a lot of blood, sweat and tears, Christian and Travis were ready to open their windows. Surviving one of the coldest winters in recent Nashville history, they are now looking forward to warmer weather. And Nashville should be looking forward to visiting their truck!

Chef Christian makes everything but the bread. He makes his own hot dogs and sausages. He hand-cuts his own chips. I will go on record and say that his barbecue hand-cut chips are probably the best I have ever had from a restaurant or food truck. He says that he gets bored easily, so when he was thinking about the concept, he wanted to make sure he had the freedom to always keep himself on his toes and always keep things fresh. In fact, there is only one mainstay item on his menu, and that is the behemoth namesake sandwich: the Confeastador. The Confeastador is a pulled-pork sandwich with spicy mustard barbecue sauce on a torta roll. It is topped with Sriracha mayo, fried onions, arugula and, finally, a fried egg. It is a beast of a sandwich!

One other menu item that pops up from time to time, and one that always draws a lot of attention, is the Foie Gras Burger. Yes, you read that right: foie gras. It's a half-pound burger topped with foie gras, red onion jam and arugula that comes with a side (normally the amazing hand-cut seasoned chips)—all priced at twelve dollars! Obviously, I'm impressed. Christian is the first one to bring foie gras to the food truck scene. But

this is the type of creativity and freedom for which he strives and to which we can look forward from the Confeastador. And it definitely sets him apart from the pack.

Another item that has been on his menu is a flatbread topped with veggies like butternut squash, mushrooms and Gruyère cheese. As the summer approaches, Chef Christian will start to go with the fruits and veggies that are in season. He says the menu will become lighter, with more salad options. You can expect some amazing fruit chutneys as well. This is basically how he chooses his menu each week: he looks at what is fresh and available, goes through his notebook of ideas that he carries with him at all times and takes it from there.

While the truck might seem fairly new, it is building a good following, and items like its popular Brisket Tacos help its growing popularity. For the Brisket Tacos, Chef Christian smokes the brisket himself for over sixteen hours. One of his favorite moments on the truck has to do with the Brisket Tacos. It was a day when a fellow truck asked the Confeastador to fill in for it at a location. This one gentleman walked up and ordered the Brisket Tacos. After he got the tacos, he wandered off, and Christian got busy making some of the other orders that were waiting. He could hear the gentleman in the background on the phone saying he was at the food truck and was eating some awesome Brisket Tacos; should he order some more to bring back to the office? The man came back up and ordered five more Brisket Tacos. Being able to see people's reactions and hearing their immediate feedback is one of the things that most owners will agree is a highlight of running a food truck.

The Confeastador is truly a chef-driven food truck to get excited about when you see it out. Christian says, "It absolutely is a chef-driven truck. I drive it every day!" You can expect unprocessed ingredients, fresh fruits and vegetables and some really extraordinary menu items. Christian and Travis both mentioned that they want a visit to their truck to be a culinary journey. They want to introduce Nashville to new things and to the foods they love and hope their customers will love as well. If you see something on the menu and you are unfamiliar with it, they'll both be happy to explain it to you and help you expand your culinary horizons. There are a lot of exciting things coming to Nashville compliments of the Confeastador truck—so be on the lookout!

To book the Conquistador at your property, office party, catered event, wedding or other event, or to just keep up with its movements, you can check out its website (www. confeastador.com), Facebook page and Twitter feed (@confeastador).

Curried Lamb Taco with Herbed Yogurt and Pickled Yellow Onions
(Recipe provided by Christian Rodrick)

For the lamb:
3 tablespoons olive oil
1 boneless leg of lam, diced into 1-inch cubes
3 tablespoons curry powder
1 tablespoon cumin
1 tablespoon coriander
1 teaspoon chile flakes
1 cup white wine
2 cups chicken stock
Salt and pepper to taste

Heat olive oil in a heavy-bottomed sauté pan. Coat the lamb with the curry powder, cumin, coriander and chile flakes. Sear the lamb in batches until golden brown. Once all the lamb is seared, take it out and set aside. Add the white wine to the pan and reduce until almost dry. Place the lamb back in the pan with the chicken stock. Simmer for about 1½ hours or until tender. Season with salt and pepper to taste.

For the onions:
1 large yellow onion

1 cup vinegar
½ cup water
½ cup sugar
¼ cup kosher salt
2 tablespoon turmeric

Julienne the yellow onion and sweat over low heat in a sauté pan until lightly softened. Combine the rest of the ingredients in a small pot and bring to a boil. Place the onions in a large mixing bowl and pour the liquid over them. Cover and let it sit for about 1 hour in the refrigerator.

For the yogurt sauce:
½ cup Greek yogurt
2 tablespoon heavy cream
2 tablespoon fresh cilantro
1 tablespoon fresh mint
Salt to taste

Mix all the ingredients in a mixing bowl.

For the flatbread:
2 ounces warm water
1 tablespoon active yeast
14 ounces bread flour
1 tablespoon honey
2 tablespoons olive oil
6 ounces cold water

Combine warm water with yeast. Let bloom for 10 minutes. Combine all ingredients in a standing mixer with a dough hook and mix until combined. Proof in a warm spot until it has doubled in size. Cut into 2-ounce portions. Roll each portion out to ¼-inch-thick rounds. Heat a sauté pan to medium-high heat. Cook each round approximately 1½ minutes on each side, until lightly browned and puffy.

To serve: Spoon lamb mixture on flatbread. Add pickled yellow onions and yogurt sauce.

CREPE A DIEM

There is an art and technique to making the perfect crêpe. Brittany Blackshear brings that art and technique to Nashville onboard the food truck Crepe A Diem.

It couldn't be more fitting for someone named Brittany to own a food truck serving crêpes since crêpes originated in Brittany, France. For those who do not know, a crêpe is basically a very thin pancake. That being said, it is in no way made like a pancake and requires a specific-style griddle or pan and equipment.

Originally a student at the Savannah College of Art and Design majoring in graphic design and print making, Brittany studied abroad in France. Starting off having only Nutella crêpes in Paris, one late night, Brittany had her first savory crêpe, and it "changed my whole perspective on the versatility." When she returned home, her family purchased for her a small electric crêpe griddle. She started off making crêpes for roommates and catered a few house parties. Then a few friends who were organizing the Earth Day Festival in Savannah, Georgia, suggested she make crêpes there. So she rented a food-vending cart that she pulled to the event

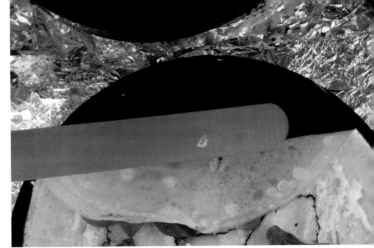

from her home. After making her mark there, she continued to cater events and small festivals for the next two years in and around Savannah. She was then ready to take the next step in her business.

That next step put Brittany under the tutelage of a Michelin-starred chef, and for the next eight months, she trained exclusively under him until she was able to perfect the art of crêpe making. Deciding to go the route of a food truck, Brittany realized Savannah was not yet ready for food trucks at the time. With family in Nashville and the food truck scene here beginning to boom, and the fact that Nashville lacked a crêpe food truck, it was a natural choice for Brittany to move here. And in 2013, Nashville was fortunate to see the opening of Crepe A Diem.

Taking full advantage of the versatility of the crêpe, Brittany is serving up everything from savory to sweet to brunch. Brittany is also a truck owner who utilizes locally sourced ingredients. So when you order the Ham and Swiss crêpe, it comes with Swiss cheese from local dairy farm Kenny's Farmhouse. When you order the Brie and Apricot crêpe, it comes with honey from local bee farmer Johnson's. When you order the Crepe Complete or Bacon Bella breakfast crêpe, it comes with an egg from local farm Pilgrim's Produce.

If you order a savory crêpe, make sure you have an appetite. The Louisiana savory crêpe is packed full of Andouille sausage, provolone cheese, caramelized onions and roasted red peppers. The spice from the sausage mixed with the creaminess of the provolone cheese, the sweetness from the onions and the smokiness from the peppers is definitely not to be taken lightly. If you're lucky, Brittany will have her Duck Confit Stuffed Apples on the menu.

Being a crêpe truck, Crepe A Diem does serve the Crepe Suzette, and it is definitely the standout on the truck (as it should be). The sweet, citrusy flavor on a perfectly created crêpe is truly a satisfying treat. If you're considering something sweet but don't want anything too filling, then put this on your to-eat list.

Some exciting things happening with Crepe A Diem in the summer of 2014 are the additions of a salamander to the truck and French baguettes to the menu. Brittany has been "hoarding" eye of the round and perfecting her roast beef recipe. So you can be on the lookout for her new baguette sandwiches. She will also be working on growing the catering side of her business.

One of the most exciting things that happened in 2013 for Crepe A Diem was at the Second Annual Nashville Street Food Awards. The truck was named the People's Choice Winner, which was based on charitable donations placed by patrons at each truck. Throughout the day, there were several categories that were blindly judged. I was lucky enough to judge the Best Taco category, and imagine my surprise when I found out at the end of the day that the winning taco (and my favorite from the entrants) was made by Crepe A Diem! Crepe A Diem took first place in the Best Taco category with a taco shell that was a fried cornmeal crêpe stuffed with duck confit, Gruyère cheese and chiffonade of mustard greens and garnished with toasted pecans and brunoise of Grand Marnier–poached local apples. Not only was the presentation beautiful, but also the flavors were phenomenal. The sweetness from the poached apples complemented the nuttiness from the pecans, which actually played well with the richness of the duck confit and Gruyère cheese. Then there was the crisp, delicious crêpe taco shell. It was inventive and executed well. And while this is not an item on Brittany's menu but was specific to this category and this event, it was a lesson to me on her extensive culinary range. It confirmed for me that she was legitimate and so was her food. Brittany also took second place in the Best Drink with her Hot Apple Cider.

The other exciting thing to happen to Crepe A Diem was that it taped a feature segment for the Cooking Channel's *Eat Street* show. This will air sometime in the spring/summer of 2014. So make sure to watch out for that and set your DVRs!

The one thing I would like people to think about when they order from Crepe A Diem is that Brittany makes everything to order on the truck. There is not a team of people preparing a generic recipe, wrapping it in paper and shooting it down a

slot. This is fresh, gourmet food that is made to order. So it might take a few extra minutes. Be patient. It's nice to know that my crêpe was made when I ordered it and wasn't sitting in a stack of crêpes for hours.

Brittany is doing classic French street crêpes. She points out that she is not trying to reinvent the wheel. The one thing she loves about the crêpe is that it is a traditional French food but is very approachable. And she wants to stay true to that. She knows what she does well, and she is sticking to that.

You can find Brittany every Saturday morning for brunch at the Franklin Farmers' Market in Franklin, Tennessee. She also can be found at Yazoo Taproom on certain Friday evenings. To keep up with her other locations throughout the week or to book catering events, you can check out Crepe A Diem's website (www.crepeadiem.com). It is also on Facebook and Twitter feed (@crepeadiem).

Crepe A Diem Crêpe Suzette
(Recipe provided by Brittany Blackshear)

This is a traditional French crêpe dessert served tableside and flambéed with Grand Marnier. This boozy, bright orange sauce is delicious on a warm, buttered crêpe and makes for an elegant dessert.
—*Brittany*

Makes 6 servings

6 frozen crêpes, thawed (or make from scratch)
2 cups sugar (plus a dash for tableside flambé)
1 ½ tablespoons unsalted butter
1 1/3 cup orange juice (freshly squeezed will take
  about 4 oranges)
½ tablespoon lemon juice
2 tablespoons orange zest
½ tablespoon lemon zest
½ cup Grand Marnier (plus a splash for tableside flambé)

If you are making your crêpes from scratch, make your 6 crêpes first. If you are not making your crêpes from scratch, you can find frozen crêpes in the freezer section of many grocery stores.

For the Suzette sauce, with a large heavy-bottomed pan on low heat, spread out the dry sugar in the pan. Do not touch. After 2 minutes, add the butter in small cubes. Let it melt untouched. Raise the heat slightly and add the lemon juice and orange juice and stir continuously until incorporated with no lumps. Let the sugar liquid start to caramelize. Watch for a light caramel color. Then add the orange and lemon zest and Grand Marnier. If you are feeling flashy, light the sauce on fire!

To serve traditionally, place each crêpe one at a time in a large frying pan with some of the Suzette sauce and turn to coat. Then fold neatly in half and fold neatly in half again so that it forms a triangle. Once they are in triangles, you can arrange several crêpes in the pan with the sauce, sprinkle some additional sugar and splash some Grand Marnier to flambé tableside!

DegThai

Jay Jenratha is the sole owner and operator of DegThai. He is also one of the most genuinely nice people I have ever met. He is appreciative of every single person who visits his truck. And he is so humble. He is serving some of *the best* Thai food in the city, and I hope you will make plans to visit him in his bright green truck featuring the most adorable of Asian cartoon children (*deg* means "children" in Thai).

Born and raised in Bangkok, Thailand, Jay learned everything he knows from his mom, who inspires him and his cooking. His favorite thing to eat is her Massaman Curry. Jay's Massaman Curry won him not only Best Sandwich at the 2012 Nashville Street Food Awards but also the 2013 Best Hot Nashville category, and his Massaman Curry Egg Roll placed second in the Best Deep-Fried category. Needless to say, if Jay's Massaman Curry is so delicious, can you imagine how good his mom's Massaman Curry must be? Here in Nashville, Jay has worked at several different Thai restaurants. The last restaurant he worked at was Royal Thai in Cool Springs, where he spent seven to eight years moving his way up from waitstaff to kitchen staff to management before deciding it was time to make food how he wanted to make food.

The idea for street food came to him for two reasons. The first and main reason is that street food is such a huge part of Thai culture. He knew he wanted to stay true to his culture. He wasn't sure at the time how to start a food truck because everyone he talked to said, "No you can't do that." And the second reason he wanted to start a food truck serving street food was because he had seen an episode of *Eat Street*. Luckily, in 2011, Jay was able to get everything organized and opened his windows. Things have been going strong and growing ever since.

Family is everything to Jay. And he started the truck so he could build something to not only provide for his family but also perhaps one day give to his daughter. It's something truly special to see him look so dotingly at his nearly two-year-old daughter (born just months after the truck opened) and his wife, who loves working on the truck with him. He jokes that they both can't wait for their daughter to grow up so they can put her to work on the truck. She always wants to help him by stirring the sauces when he cooks at home, so he's trying to help her fall in love with food at a young age.

The same care and devotion he has with family he brings to his truck. Because of the limitations of the truck in terms of the setup and equipment, his menu is restricted. He would love to have a wok on the truck, but space limitations and also a snafu in the setup when he got the truck have made that impossible. A long-term goal is to eventually grow into a brick and mortar of sorts. He does not want a full restaurant but more of a "DegThai Express," something along the lines of a more carry-out-style establishment. And he'd like to someday replace the current truck with a new truck that has the proper setup for a wok.

There is a reason Jay's Massaman Curry wins so many awards. It is truly one of my favorite things to order off his truck, whether it's the Massaman Curry Beef Plate or the Massaman Curry Wrap. One thing I do want to mention is that there is a difference between Thai curry flavors and Indian curry flavors. While they have some similar components, they also have some different components, and the flavors (at least to me) are very different. I've met people who immediately say no to the Massaman Curry, the Green Curry or the Red Curry from the truck based solely on the word "curry" because they are not fans of Indian curries. Jim, for example, could eat DegThai's Green Curry pretty much all day long, yet he's not a huge fan of Indian curry. All that is to say: don't count out the Massaman Curry based on the word curry.

Just in the last year, Jay added Pad Thai, perhaps the most popular and well-known Thai dish, to his menu. Note to everyone in Nashville: The Pad Thai will take a bit longer than any of the truck's other menu items because there is so much involved in the making and preparation of this dish that cannot be done until it's ordered. And every time you order, it is made fresh—it isn't sitting around in some steamer. This is great food, not fast food. Jay prides himself that his Pad Thai is comparable to what you would find at any street vendor in Bangkok. He hasn't watered down any flavors to make them more likeable to mainstream America. He is making truly genuine Thai Pad Thai.

If that isn't enough, his egg rolls are both familiar in concept to the Nashville public and amazing in taste. By all means, dip the egg rolls in the sauce that comes with the order. There is a reason the egg rolls come with a sauce. While they might seem a little small, they actually are perfectly portioned when you also order a sandwich or entrée. The egg rolls are perfectly sized as an appetizer. They are not meant to be a meal.

Thai food is meant to be spicy. Jay keeps the spice level to a fairly tame level. If you like the heat kicked up, just let him know when you order.

One thing that helps complement the spiciness is the DegThai Thai Tea. It's truly stupendous. And it is really thirst quenching on a hot day. It's worth the couple of dollars it costs. It's the Thai version of sweet tea. At its basic core, Thai tea is sweetened tea mixed with coconut milk. But there are actually more spices mixed in, and every Thai establishment has its own blend of spices. So while they might taste similar, no two establishments will ever have identical-tasting Thai teas. I know several people, food truck owners and food truck patrons alike, who visit DegThai strictly because they are addicted to Jay's Thai tea. Because of the coconut milk that is mixed in with the tea, it is also a good drink to have on hand when you are eating something spicy from the truck.

Jay mentioned that he is constantly explaining to people who visit the truck what Thai food is. If you aren't familiar with Thai food, allow Jay and DegThai to introduce you. Let him expand your taste buds and culinary horizons. DegThai does have a few regular spots. On most Thursday nights, you can find it down near the 100 Oaks area of Nashville at Tobacco Road Coffee & Smoke Shop from 5:00 to 9:00 p.m. It can also be found on most Saturdays at Friedman's Army/Navy Store, located on Twenty-first Avenue in the Hillsboro Village area of Nashville, from 11:00 a.m. to 5:00 p.m. On Sundays, it can be found at one of two spots: McKay Used Books off Old Hickory Boulevard out in Bellevue on the west side of Nashville or off Twenty-fourth Avenue at Vanderbilt Row on the Vanderbilt Campus from noon until 9:00 p.m. or until Jay sells out.

To keep up with DegThai's other locations throughout the week or to book it at your private event, you can check out its website (www.degthai.com), Facebook page (DegThai.Jay) or Twitter feed (@DegThaiTruck).

DegThai's Massaman Curry Beef
(Recipe provided by Jay Jenratha)

Start with curry paste (or you can get instant Massaman curry paste at most Asian markets):
¼ cup garlic
3 shallots
5 dried whole chiles, seeds and stems removed

½ cup lemongrass, thinly sliced
4 pods cardamom
1 cinnamon stick
5 cloves
1 tablespoons coriander
$^1/_3$ tablespoon cumin
½ cup galangal (blue ginger), sliced
$^1/_3$ tablespoon peppercorns
1 tablespoon salt
1 mace
1 nutmeg
1 teaspoon shrimp paste

In a large frying pan on medium-high heat, roast the garlic and shallots with skin on. Roast until the skin is burned and the flesh is soft and cooked. It should take about 5 to 10 minutes. Remove them from the heat and cool. When the garlic and shallots are cooled, peel the skin and remove any burned spots, then set aside for the pounding process.

In a large frying pan, toast the chiles and lemongrass until slightly brown. It should take about 2 or 3 minutes. Remove from heat and let them cool for the pounding process.

In a large frying pan, place the remaining spices, except for the shrimp paste, and toast them by moving them around the pan until they are fragrant. Then take them off the heat to cool for the pounding process.

Pounding Process:
In a large mortar and pestle, start with the chiles and the salt. When the chiles are roughly ground, add the lemongrass. Pound until the lemongrass is roughly ground. Add the rest of the spices, except for the roasted garlic, shallots and shrimp paste. Pound until well blended. This can take up to 30 minutes. Add the roasted garlic, shallots and shrimp paste. Pound until everything is smoothly ground. Massaman Curry Paste should be dark red and smoothly ground. Keep refrigerated.

For Massaman Curry Beef:
10 pounds beef knuckle, cut into 1-inch cubes
2 cups Massaman Curry Paste

1,200 milliliters coconut milk (three 400-milliliter cans of
coconut milk split 200 and 1,000)
1 pound potatoes, cut in 1½-inch cubes
4 tablespoon tamarind juice
1½ tablespoon salt
7 tablespoons palm sugar
½ cup roasted peanuts

Add beef to a pot. Cover the beef with water and bring to a
boil. Once the water comes to a boil, turn down to simmer at
medium heat for 3 hours, uncovered. At the end of 3 hours,
there should be a little water left in the pot, and the beef should
be tender. Set aside.

In large pan, add the Massaman Curry Paste and 200 milliliters
of coconut milk. Cook on low heat for 10 minutes. You should
see some red oil floating (from the coconut milk and paste).
Then pour this into the pot with your beef.

Put your pot with beef back on the stovetop. Add the rest of
the coconut milk, potatoes, tamarind juice and salt and bring
to a boil. Then simmer on low heat for 30 minutes, uncovered.

Add the palm sugar and peanuts. Keep on low heat for
another 30 minutes. The Massaman Curry should be thickened,
with a beautiful red oil floating on top. The toasted peanuts
will be soft. When the curry is fragrant with spices and toasted
nuts, it means it is "ready to serve." Serve with steamed rice or
toasted bread.

*According to Jay, there are three flavors that need to balance: sweet, salty and sour. The
Massaman Curry should be more salty than sweet. The sour should be the last flavor that you
taste and the least intense.

Delta Bound

Delta Bound holds a special place in my heart. When I started my blog, the first truck I reviewed was Delta Bound. And as fate would have it, it was the truck's inaugural day out—the first time its window had ever been open for business. I remember it was the first time I had ever tasted a fried bologna sandwich. There were a lot of firsts that happened that day. Through the last two years, I have had the opportunity to get to know Jess and Stacey more, and I've been fortunate enough to eat from their truck quite often.

Being from the Louisiana Delta region, Jessica and Stacey Mobley obviously lean toward Cajun and Creole flavors. But I was surprised to learn that they also have a strong influence of Texas barbecue. It is one of the things they do well on their truck. They are able to properly fuse the Cajun and Creole influences together with southern barbecue. They make these flavors complement, not clash with, one another.

Chef Jess started out in the culinary field in pastry. She wanted to decorate cakes and not only took classes but also taught classes in pastry. For a time, she did have her own business making wedding cakes as well. And then she fell into the savory world, working in a kitchen. She was starting to feel that she was done working in someone else's kitchen and was ready to work in her own. Jess took the idea of a food truck to Stacey, who initially thought it was a crazy idea. With Stacey doing extensive research, Jess quit her job in April 2012, and the truck hit the streets in May.

While Jess takes charge of the kitchen and recipes, Stacey is enamored of meat and smoking meats. After reading book after book and having conversations with numerous people, Stacey began experimenting with different meats, different temperatures and

different rubs. So Stacey has taken the time, care and love to smoke to perfection all of the smoked meats offered on the truck. In fact, Delta Bound was one of the first trucks to start serving brisket. Two years ago, there wasn't a lot of brisket on the non-barbecue savory trucks. Now, when you walk around at a food truck event, nearly every savory truck has brisket in some form on its menu, from tacos to chili to sandwiches. Delta Bound was one of the first. In fact, at the Inaugural Nashville Street Food Awards in 2012 (a mere three months after Delta Bound opened), Delta Bound's Smoked Brisket Sliders won first place in the Best Barbecue category. Stacey is now looking into making his own hot dogs, sausage and even bologna. They really are trying to have as much control over what goes into their food as possible.

A favorite item that I *always* order when it's on the menu is the Catfish Tacos. I'm serious when I say that I always order these when they are on the menu. In fact, Jim has been known to place two orders of the Catfish Tacos. You get two tacos in an order, and each taco has the perfect portion of filling. Each taco has two perfectly breaded and fried strips of catfish topped with fresh sweet corn salsa, and then the Delta Bound Comeback Sauce is drizzled on top. This taco has ridiculous flavor. The breading is perfect so that you get that great crispiness, but it doesn't overpower or cover the taste of the catfish. The sweet corn salsa complements the naturally mild taste of the catfish. And that Comeback Sauce on top—are you kidding me? Because Delta Bound does as much as possible from scratch, the Catfish Tacos are relegated to summer when sweet corn is in season. So as the summer arrives, be on the lookout for the Catfish Tacos. They were the runner-up for Best Taco at the 2012 Nashville Street Food Awards.

At a recent major Mardi Gras event in downtown Nashville, one of the favorite dishes among both the patrons and fellow food truck owners, as well as one of the first items to be sold out, was the Crawfish Étouffée. Luckily, Jess was kind enough to share that recipe with us (see pages 48–49).

Because of Jess's pastry past, the desserts are not to be missed. No matter how full I am from savory food, I'll still order Jess's desserts, even if I have to take them home before I can find room to eat them. Her Peach Empanadas with Caramel Sauce are some of the best sweet food truck items I've ever had. In fact, her caramel sauce is a standout in any dessert she uses it in. She uses the caramel sauce in her Caramel Corn Pot de Crème, which took third place at the 2013 Nashville Street Food Awards in the Best Dessert category. The I Want S'More Whiskey Pudding took second place in the Best Olive & Sinclair category. But it isn't just the sweets where her pastry past makes a mark. When they have muffuletta sandwiches on the menu, Jess and Stacey make the muffuletta bread themselves. So every bit of that sandwich, bread included, is made from scratch.

Speaking of the Nashville Street Food Awards, Delta Bound also won second place in the Best Hot Nashville category in 2013 for its Spicy BBQ Chicken and Hushpuppy Waffle.

In 2014, Delta Bound was another one of the trucks that the Cooking Channel's *Eat Street* filmed for a feature to be aired in the spring/summer. I was lucky enough to be able to sneak away from my day job to head down to Yazoo Brewery and Taproom for the taping. It's an awkward experience to have someone tape you eating, let me tell you. But it's a small price to pay so that Delta Bound can get some national recognition—recognition it truly does deserve!

Showing their versatility, Chef Jess and Stacey recently completed a semi pop-up dinner event with Yazoo Brewery and Taproom as part of the brewery's "Cooking with Yazoo" series. The premise is that beer is incorporated into each course of the four-course dinner. Again, Jess and Stacey stayed true to their roots and really gave us some fantastic Cajun/Creole food while incorporating that southern flair. From beer-braised pork hot tamales to stuffed collards, Jess and Stacey are really making a name for themselves and solidifying their place in the top tier of food trucks here in Nashville.

To find the truck, inquire about catering or keep up with Jess and Stacey's goings-on, you can check their website (www.delta-bound.com), Facebook page or Twitter feed (@DeltaBoundTN).

Delta Bound's Crawfish Étouffée
(Recipe provided by Jessica Mobley)

Yields 2 quarts/8 servings

¼ pound unsalted butter
2½ cups "the Holy Trinity": onion, celery and bell
  pepper, diced
½ cup diced tomato
2 tablespoon garlic, minced
2 bay leaves
1 cup flour
2 pounds Louisiana crawfish tails*
½ cup tomato sauce
2 cups crawfish stock (can substitute shrimp or chicken
  stock; plus up to 1 cup separately, as needed)

Salt and cayenne pepper to taste
Louisiana hot sauce to taste
½ cup green onions sliced

In a heavy pot, melt the butter and cook "the Holy Trinity," diced tomato, garlic and bay leaves until vegetables are wilted. Stir in flour constantly until a white roux is achieved.

Blend crawfish tails and tomato sauce into mixture and cook for 5 minutes, stirring to prevent scorching.

Slowly add the crawfish stock until a thick sauce-like consistency is achieved. Bring to a rolling boil, then reduce to a simmer and cook for 30 minutes. Add more stock as needed to retain consistency.

Season to taste with salt, cayenne pepper and hot sauce. To serve, spoon over hot rice and garnish with green onions and a slice of French bread on the side.

*Note from Jess: Please support southern agriculture by buying U.S. crawfish.

Delta Bound's Caramel Sauce
(Recipe Provided by Jessica Mobley)

Yields 3 cups

1 pound sugar
1 teaspoon lemon juice
2 tablespoons cane syrup (or corn syrup)
2 ounces unsalted butter
1½ cups heavy cream
½ teaspoon salt

Combine sugar, lemon juice and syrup in a small saucepan. Bring to a boil and cook on medium heat until the color becomes a deep amber. Remove from heat and stir in the butter and cream. Add salt, stirring well. Let mixture come to room temperature. Store in the refrigerator. This sauce is great on desserts of all kinds!

DOUGHWORKS & LOCO DONUTS

Nick Moeller is the owner and operator of the Doughworks food truck. This truck has evolved so much from the time that it originally opened on February 1, 2013. In the late summer of 2013, the truck reemerged in a new vehicle with a rebranded logo and a truly spectacular from-scratch doughnut.

After looking into a different concept for a brick and mortar and realizing financially that it was out of the realm of possibility, Nick began looking into the booming Nashville food truck scene. Realizing that there were not really any breakfast trucks, and especially doughnut trucks, Nick began to put together a business plan. The inspiration behind the concept of doughnuts stems from Nick's lifetime obsession with the tasty treat.

The original concept for Doughworks had the doughnut trying to be a lot more than a doughnut. Luckily for us, Nick came to the decision that Doughworks is both a breakfast and a doughnut truck. The doughnut is going to be a doughnut—and an awesome doughnut at that! Inspired by Gourdough's in Austin, Texas (you might have seen it on *Eat Street*), Nick is making small batches of from-scratch doughnuts on the truck. This means the doughnuts are made to order. Your doughnut has not been sitting in a display case for hours upon hours. That freshly cooked doughnut is then topped with some creative and completely mouth-watering homemade sauce and topping combinations.

The goal in the next year for Doughworks is to continue bringing quality and delicious doughnuts to the streets of Nashville while also building into the schedule some major events like the Counterpoint Music Festival in Georgia. Nick wants to be able to serve at three or four major festivals a year. The ultimate long-term goal doesn't find Nick taking Doughworks along the route to a brick and mortar. He absolutely loves the community of food trucks and the feel of being in the truck. He says that he would like to see Doughworks expand to other cities with similar feels to Nashville, where the food trucks are widely accepted and the city legislators and tourism boards aren't causing code and permit headaches.

One of the things I appreciate so much about Nick is that he really takes any and all feedback to heart. When you eat at his truck, let him know what you think. He takes that feedback to make his business, his product and his selections better. What the customer thinks actually matters to Nick. I've never seen anyone smile bigger than Nick when I take a bite of one of his doughnuts and give him the "winner-winner-doughnut-dinner" look. It is also important to Nick to give back. Working with several nonprofits, he donates his time and sometimes his doughnuts in an effort to help make Nashville a brighter and better place to call home.

There are a few things that make Doughworks stand apart from so many of the doughnut joints around town. The first is that these are from-scratch doughnuts.

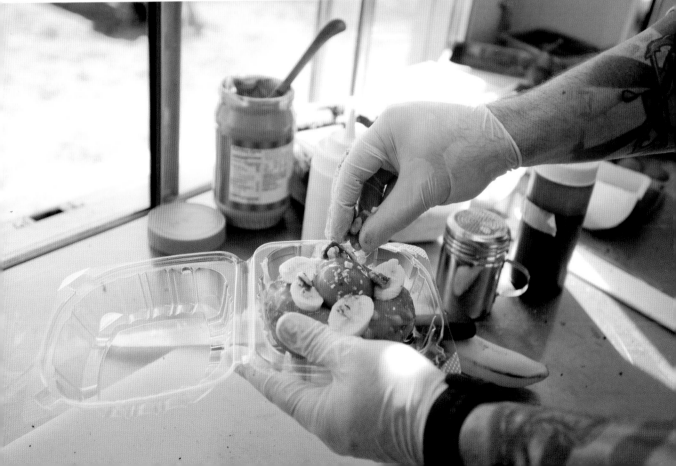

Nick proofs the doughnuts before they are fried and made into deliciousness. There is a very small market that actually makes from-scratch doughnuts, without using a mix. And because of how Nick makes his doughnuts procedurally, the customer gets a very hearty doughnut. While at a doughnut joint, you could probably order and eat three, four, five or a half dozen doughnuts and spend maybe four or five dollars, they never feel satisfying because they are basically glazed pieces of air. Doughworks doughnuts are satisfying. One Doughworks doughnut will far surpass the experience and enjoyment that any sixty-cent doughnut could ever hope to give you!

In 2013, Doughworks grew and acquired the Loco Donuts brand. The Loco Donuts food truck was creating mini doughnuts and making gourmet sundae-type creations with these doughnuts. Loco Donuts closed during the summer of 2013, and Doughworks, through many talks, has now added the brand and equipment to its offerings. Upon request and at special events, customers have available the mini doughnut option (although the mini doughnuts are not made from scratch, as they require different equipment and a different process). So it is a one-two punch of awesomeness! Doughworks offers an excellent from-scratch doughnut but now has the capability, on special occasions, to appeal to the mini doughnut fan base as well. The brand remains Doughworks, but it is now "Proudly serving Loco Donuts."

When you order a doughnut from Doughworks, the doughnut is dropped into the oil to cook at that time. And, oh yeah, you also get the doughnut hole! The truck's menu offers a range of toppings, from the Yazoo Special, which has a Yazoo "Gerst" Amber Ale Caramel sauce with crumbled bacon, to the Black Cadillac, which has cocoa cream, crumbled brownie, brownie batter and powdered sugar. It also has weekly specialties, which might be a crème brûlée doughnut or a Doughworks doughnut topped with peanut butter cups.

I asked Nick where he got the inspiration for his topping creations. He smiled big and replied, "I have a *crazy* sweet tooth. I can make all these concoctions and know that they taste good together because that is what I love to eat! Like the brownie and the brownie batter on the Black Cadillac or the strawberries and cream in the Strawberry Field."

During my most recent trip to Doughworks, I decided not to get one of its toppings but to instead try the powdered sugar doughnut. Nick takes the from-scratch scratch doughnut and shakes it in powdered sugar until it is completely covered. It was pretty awesome because by the time we got the doughnut home, since the doughnut was warm when he covered it, the powdered sugar (while still powdery and white) had also partly turned into a delicious glaze. It was like a truly spectacular glazed doughnut, but with unparalleled substance and flavor

From the plain cinnamon sugar and powdered sugar doughnuts to those that are topped with inventive ingredients, Doughworks is starting off the mornings in and around Nashville on a sweet note. It is now serving Humphrey's Street Coffee as well. So you can grab that doughnut and coffee on your way in to work each day. To find the truck, schedule a private catering or invite Doughworks to your property, check out its website (www.doughworksnashville.com), Facebook page (Doughworks Nashville) and Twitter feed (@DoughworksTruck).

Doughworks Yazoo "Gerst" Amber Ale Caramel
(Recipe provided by Nick Moeller)

Yield: 27 ounces / Portion size: 1 ounce
Preparation time: 5 minutes / Cooking time: 15 minutes

6 ounces Yazoo "Gerst" Amber Ale
Water as needed

1 pound granulated sugar
2 ounces unsalted butter
8 ounces heavy cream
½ tablespoon salt, sea or kosher

Pour beer into large saucepan with a pinch of salt and turn on high heat until it begins to simmer. Turn heat to medium and simmer until beer reduces by a third and is flat. Turn off heat and set aside.

In a separate large saucepan, add just enough water to hydrate the sugar (about ½ cup). Place over medium heat and gently stir until sugar dissolves. Once the sugar starts to simmer, stop stirring and turn heat to high. With water, brush down any ice crystals on the side of the saucepan as needed. Do not stir again until desired caramelization is reached.

Watch the sugar as it begins to caramelize (288 degrees) until a dark tan color is reached. Turn off the heat, add the butter and whisk until incorporated.

Add heavy cream to caramel and whisk until the sugar stops bubbling

Add the beer and salt and mix until incorporated. Place in a metal container and put in the freezer or an ice bath to rapidly cool. Once the temperature is reduced, place in a container, cover with plastic wrap and refrigerate.

THE GRILLED CHEESERIE

While Mas Tacos Por Favor is widely acknowledged as the first true gourmet food truck in Nashville, the Grilled Cheeserie was the one to put the food truck into the mainstream here in the city. Let me just say that if the Grilled Cheeserie had come out and done things differently, the landscape of the Nashville food truck scene would also be drastically different. This section is my attempt at an ode to the Grilled Cheeserie to say thank you!

If you are in Nashville and do not know of the Grilled Cheeserie, you must be new to the area (like you've been here less than twenty-four hours), or you must live under a rock.

Just as it was for thousands upon thousands of people in middle Tennessee, as I already mentioned in my introduction, the Grilled Cheeserie was my very first food truck experience. The only thing that has kept me from visiting the truck more often is what I call the "Grilled Cheeserie Line." You know what I'm talking about. The other food truck owners know what I'm talking about. The Grilled Cheeserie knows what I'm talking about. I've been lucky to catch the truck on a few occasions when the line was short (these are the only times I am thankful that Nashvillians are fair-weather food truck patrons).

I feel as though each time I eat from the Grilled Cheeserie truck, the food has gotten tastier than the last time. I'm a life-long pickle hater. I've been known to send food back at restaurants because there was a pickle on the plate. I've even been that girl who lied and told the waiter that I was allergic to pickles when ordering food to help ensure that there would not be a pickle on my plate. But the last time I visited the Grilled Cheeserie, I was handed some house-made pickles. This year, I made a goal for myself to really expand my taste buds and vowed to retry things that I previously hadn't cared for. So I slowly placed one of the Grilled Cheeserie's pickles into my mouth and ate it. And to my shock, I liked it! In fact, I ate two more slices of the pickle, which, at Jim's suggestion, I wrapped around a tator tot. (This combination is surprisingly good. The salt from the tator tot really complements the pickle.) So the Grilled Cheeserie got me to eat and like pickles. Mad respect!

The Grilled Cheeserie is the ever so popular creation of Le Cordon Bleu chef Crystal de Luna-Bogan and her husband, Joseph Bogan. The only reason I am going to mention that they are both California transplants is because the food truck scene had already been around for years in that area before they moved. Crystal has several family members who all run successful food trucks out in California. One of the hard things about starting up a food truck is knowing exactly how to get started, what kind of truck to buy, how to set it up and how to develop a concept. If Crystal and Joseph had not been the ones to start the first mainstream Nashville food truck, the landscape of this industry in the city would be drastically different. I think it would

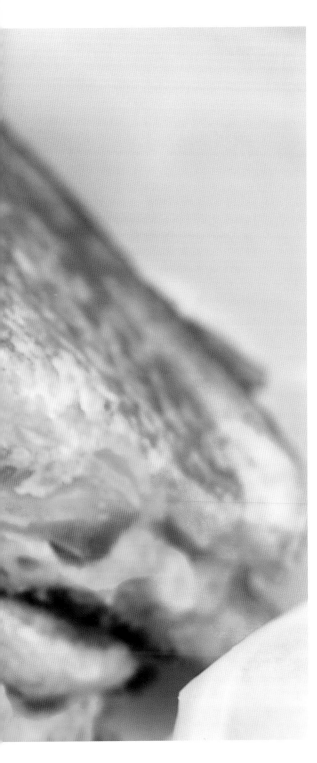

have taken at least a year longer for the food truck story to emerge if they had not had the family resources to guide them through the pitfalls every new truck can fall into.

Another reason I say this is because of Crystal's skill. She really is absolutely ridiculous in a kitchen. OK, truth be told, I've never actually seen her working in a kitchen outside her truck, but when I eat the flavors she creates between those two pieces of grilled bread, I can tell she is beyond talented. Joseph even jokes that he'll look in their fridge at home and think they have nothing for dinner. Crystal will walk in there, and moments later, a delicious dinner is served.

The definition of grilled cheese is a cheese sandwich that is grilled until the cheese is gooey and melted and the bread is a golden brown bit of buttery, crispy deliciousness. We can all agree on that, right? But this is not two slices of discount generic-brand grocery store bread with a slice of vegetable oil cheese in between. This is bread from local bakeries, cheese from the best dairy farms in the area, Benton's bacon and meats from Porter Road Butcher. Not only are Crystal and Joseph utilizing the best, freshest ingredients possible, but also Crystal does everything from scratch. While I don't believe she is making the macaroni for the Pimento Mac 'n' Cheese sandwich, it genuinely would not surprise me if she did!

In my first experience with the Grilled Cheeserie, I think I enjoyed the concept of the food truck more than the food because I don't remember what I had other than that it had a fried egg on it. It didn't leave a lasting impression on me like the Pimento Mac 'n' Cheese did. And I couldn't be more happy that Crystal chose to share that recipe with us for this book. In the South, pimento cheese is nearly an institution. You find it in a lot of places, but everyone has his or her own take on it. Or maybe it's just the process they use to make their pimento cheese more than the actual ingredients. Regardless, having to share that Pimento Mac 'n' Cheese sandwich was probably one of the hardest things I've ever had to do. Who doesn't love macaroni and cheese? Who doesn't love grilled cheese? Put them together and—wow! And let's not forget that this sandwich also adds Benton's (phenomenal) bacon. This sandwich won third place at the 2013 Nashville Street Food Awards in the Best Between Bread category.

Each season, Crystal and Joseph feature three sandwiches and then add in their weekly "Melt of the Moment." So each week, there's a new melt, and every few months, there's a whole new menu. Crystal's soups are really flavorful as well. The roasted red pepper and tomato soup has a strong smoky flavor, almost similar to barbecue sauce. This soup was half of their second-place Best Vegetarian entry at the Nashville Street Food Awards. The other half was their Autumn Grilled Cheese sandwich with Brie, kale, pumpkinseed pesto and roasted butternut squash.

One of their spring 2014 menu items is called the B&B. It has Benton's bacon, buttermilk cheddar and peach jam on multigrain bread. There is something about the sweet flavor from the fruit mixed with the saltiness of the bacon and the creaminess of the cheddar that I just love.

If you just want a good old nod to your childhood, you can make your own melt. You pick your bread. You pick your cheese. You pick any additional ingredients. And if you are watching your gluten, they do have gluten-free bread available. Vegan? They have vegan rice milk cheese.

So why did Crystal and Joseph decide on a grilled cheese truck? Well, first off, Crystal loves cheese. I'm not talking a little bit. She. Loves. Cheese. Also, the grilled cheese is something that is recognizable and familiar to everyone. And yet, it leaves itself open to new and spectacular versions that allow Crystal and Joseph to be creative and utilize Crystal's culinary background—a background that includes extensive experience at fine-dining establishments like Southern California's Napa Rose, the Four Seasons Hotel in Beverly Hills and Los Angeles's Clementine.

If you want a grilled cheese, they can do that. But while what they serve is technically called grilled cheese, what you actually get is so much more than that. The Grilled Cheeserie is, hands down, the most popular truck in Nashville. It has been named the *Nashville Scene*'s Best Food Truck for three years running and the *Tennessean*'s Best Food Truck for the last two years. And it has placed in or won multiple categories at the Nashville Street Food Awards. As if that weren't enough, it was recently featured on an episode of Guy Fieri's *Diner's, Drive-Ins and Dives* on the Food Network.

Obviously, since the Grilled Cheeserie is such a popular truck, if you have a private event or catering need, it is best to contact Crystal and Joseph months in advance. They are out most Tuesdays through Saturdays and sometimes on Sundays. To catch their schedule or request a private catering or booking, you can visit their website (www.thegrilledcheeserietruck.com), Facebook page (the Grilled Cheeserie Truck) or Twitter feed (@GrlldCheeserie).

The Grilled Cheeserie's Pimento Mac 'n' Cheese
(Recipe provided by Crystal de Luna-Bogan)

Yields 4 sandwiches

Mac 'n' Cheese mix:
1 clove garlic, smashed and chopped
1 teaspoon Frank's Red Hot hot sauce or hot sauce of
   your choice
½ teaspoon cayenne pepper
1 teaspoon paprika
Fresh cracked pepper to taste
1 teaspoon kosher salt (might need more depending on
   which cheese is used)
1 cup Hellman's or Best Foods mayonnaise (The Grilled
   Cheeserie makes its own mayonnaise.* If desired, replace
   the mayo with 1 egg and 1 cup vegetable or grape seed
   oil, just not olive oil.)
4 ounces shredded smoked cheddar**
4 ounces shredded cheddar**
1 cup macaroni pasta, cooked and cooled
1 roasted bell pepper, small and diced

*If you choose to make your own mayonnaise from scratch (good
for you!), you can add the egg with your spice and garlic. In a food
processor, blend together well, and while the processor is running,
slowly drizzle in the oil.
**If you prefer a less smoky flavor, you can use all cheddar or any
shredded cheese available, like Colby or pepper jack.

In a food processor, blend together garlic, hot sauce, cayenne, paprika, black pepper and kosher salt. Then add mayo and shredded cheese and pulse until combined. Put mixture in a bowl and fold in cooked macaroni pasta and roasted red bell pepper. Season to taste.

Sandwich components:
2 slices country white bread (we use local Slikie's bread),
   buttered generously
2 thick slices of tomato
1 piece bacon, diced and cooked (we use Benton's bacon)
2 ounces mild cheddar cheese

To assemble sandwich, heat a nonstick griddle to about 300 degrees or medium-high heat. Place one slice of the generously buttered bread, butter side down, on the griddle. Spread about ½ cup of the mac 'n' cheese mix on the bread, then add the 2 slices of tomato, bacon and smoked cheddar. Place the other slice of bread on top with the butter side up. Grill on both sides until the bread is golden brown.

HOSS' LOADED BURGERS

I love burgers. I am almost a meat-a-holic. I could eat a version of a burger for breakfast, lunch and dinner. So when I first saw Hoss' Loaded Burgers out, I hoped against hope that it was a good burger. The meat juice that dripped on my shirt that day was only one indicator that it, indeed, was.

Dallas Shaw, owner and operator of Hoss' Loaded Burgers, comes to us from the business world. Touted by the Nashville food truck world as the "Most Organized Food Truck Owner," he could tell you exactly how many burgers he's ever sold, which kinds and precisely what he's sold at every event since he's opened his windows. He can use this to spot trends, helping him determine what sells best in each area of town or at big events. It's a methodical approach, but it's one that has made Hoss' Loaded Burgers extremely successful. The truck has even been featured on the Cooking Channel's *Eat Street*.

Nashville is chock-full of burger joints. It's kind of the new trend: the gourmet burger joint. But Dallas was on the forefront of that trend, having opened Hoss' in 2011. He was also one of the originals on the food truck circuit.

Having always loved food, Dallas actually wanted to go to culinary school after high school. But at the insistence of his parents, he pursued a degree in business administration and then his MBA. Throughout this time, he worked in a pastry kitchen in St. Louis and in the kitchens at several chain restaurants, all the while gaining experience in the food world. After working in the business world at two different huge conglomerates (one of which brought him to Nashville), Dallas got tired of filling out report after report after report. He began to extensively research options of entering the food world. Inspired by a stuffed burger concept he saw on a TV show on the Food Network, Dallas's original concept was for a pretty neat brick-and-mortar establishment. And in the interest that he might one day still decide to do this, I will not divulge what that burger joint concept was. That being said, trying to come up with the half-million-dollar collateral for a brick-and-mortar restaurant was just too much for him. After attending an Art Crawl event in downtown Nashville, Dallas saw the Grilled Cheeserie. This led him to do some more research, this time on food trucks. After developing his business plan, he got his truck loan two months later, and about one month after that, Hoss' Loaded Burgers was serving up cheesy, juicy, delicious burgers on the streets of Nashville.

THE TRUCKS

So how did he decide on the name Hoss' Loaded Burgers? Well, there is actually a cute little story there. The story goes that when Dallas was young, his dad told him a story about how he once had a boss who called him "Hoss," "lad" or "boy." And for whatever reason, Dallas's dad began to call Dallas Hoss, lad or boy, or run them together as "Hoss Lad Boy." Sometime later, Dallas came across a letter from his grandmother in which she had written about Dallas owning his own burger place called Big D's Burgers. Now, she wrote this letter long before Dallas ever opened Hoss', so it's clear that having a burger establishment has been a long time coming for him. Unfortunately, the Big D's name was already taken. So as he began to think up names, Dallas remembered how his dad had called him Hoss as a child. He originally was looking at Hoss' Stuffed Burgers, but there were just so many *s*'s there that it got a little confusing. So thinking of synonyms for stuffed, the word "loaded" came to mind. Hoss' Loaded Burgers—HLB—Hoss Lad Boy. It's a bit of homage to his childhood and to his dad. And there you have the story behind the name of Hoss' Loaded Burgers.

Now, back in 2012, Dallas tweeted about a new burger for which he was looking for a name. It had Muenster cheese on it with arugula and truffle aioli. The first name that popped in my head was Herman Munster from *The Addams Family*. So I tweeted over "The Herman." I'm sure that many Nashvillians tweeted the same idea. And low and behold, he did name the burger "The Herman." So this burger has a special place in my heart. Plus, Muenster cheese is one of my favorites.

The two burgers that are mainstays on his menu are the Old-Timer and the Hoss. The Old-Timer is your most familiar of burgers. Stuffed with cheddar cheese, the Old-Timer is topped with ketchup, onion, mustard, lettuce and tomato. The Hoss is also stuffed with cheddar cheese and topped with Benton's bacon, smoky barbecue sauce, cilantro and onion crispers.

His other two or maybe three burgers on the menu rotate. He tries to keep each on for one or two months at a time, so every month there is at least one burger rotating off and one burger rotating on. If you love one of the specialty burgers, make sure to keep up with the Hoss' menu on its website and Twitter feed. Once a burger rotates off, it might be several months or maybe a year before that burger will return to the menu. So get your fix before it rotates off!

All Dallas's burgers are one-third-pound grass-fed beef. He also offers a vegan soy patty. He does fries in two ways: Parmesan or Cajun. Me? I'm a sucker for the Cajun seasoning! One thing to keep in mind: the serving of fries is more than you think. When I order a burger from Dallas, I can't eat the whole burger and an entire small order of fries. If there are two of you and you are going to split the fries, you could probably split a large. My boyfriend and I, well, we split a small. You can always add extra cheese, bacon or even a fried egg to your burger. And if you're monstrously hungry, you can order a double Hoss' Loaded Burger and get a second stuffed patty!

From his Red, White and Bleu burger and his Buffalo burger to the Italian Job, his pizza-style burger with some Porter Road Butcher sausage mixed in, Dallas is able to keep the menu fresh and delicious. He is even now still working on some new burger recipes that might one day work their way onto the menu.

One of the coolest experiences I've ever had at Hoss' Loaded Burger was in the summer of 2013 at a Friday Night food truck event over in East Nashville. A group of gentleman walked up to the truck and started taking pictures. We later learned that a well-known Argentinean musician was in that group and told his friends that he *had* to visit Hoss' Loaded Burgers because he had seen it on TV. To see the look on the faces of Dallas and his employee that night—pure excitement—was so incredible. They were just as excited to meet the musician as he was to eat from their truck. There was a lot of picture taking and a lot of smiles. To know that you created a concept that speaks not only to the immediate Nashville area and its residents but also to people thousands of miles away who make a trip to your truck part of their vacation plans—it's an amazing thing. It was an exciting encounter for me to witness. The smile on Dallas's face the rest of the night was probably the biggest I've ever seen it.

One tip from this food truck junkie: the burgers are juicy, and the cheese will ooze out. So if you are wearing clothes you don't want meat juice to drip on, eat with caution. To me, burger stains on clothes are almost a badge of honor!

To follow Dallas and Hoss' Loaded Burgers, look at its menu, check its weekly locations or book it for a private catering or corporate park, visit its website (www.hossburgers.com), Facebook page or Twitter feed (@hossburgers). Because it is one of the more popular trucks in Nashville, you should consider booking it months in advance for events. Even one month out can be too last minute!

Dallas's Favorite Baja Fish Tacos
(Recipe provided by Dallas Shaw)

Yields 8 servings
Preparation: 30 minutes / Cook time: 5 minutes per batch

1 cup reduced-fat ranch salad dressing
3 tablespoons adobo sauce
2 tablespoons fresh cilantro, minced
2 tablespoons lime juice
2 pounds mahi-mahi, cut into 1-inch strips
¼ teaspoon salt
¼ teaspoon pepper
²/₃ cup all-purpose flour
3 eggs, beaten
2 cups panko (Japanese) breadcrumbs
1 cup canola oil
16 corn tortillas (6-inch), warmed
3 cups cabbage, shredded
Additional minced fresh cilantro and lime wedges

In a small bowl, combine the salad dressing, adobo sauce, cilantro and lime juice. Chill until serving.

Sprinkle mahi-mahi with salt and pepper. Place the flour, eggs and breadcrumbs in their own separate shallow bowls. Coat the mahi-mahi with flour, then dip in the eggs and finally dip into the breadcrumbs. In a large skillet, heat oil over medium heat; cook the fish in batches for 2 to 3 minutes on each side or until golden brown. Drain on paper towels.

Place fish in tortillas; top with cabbage, sauce mixture and additional cilantro; and serve with lime wedges.

THE MOBILE CHEF

Gordon Sympson did Nashville a huge favor. He loved to cook. He loved home-cooked meals, and he loved to create them for his kids. He traveled and introduced his sons to international cuisines from Spain to Mexico to many places in between. What he did was create a family culture around the love of food—and not just food, but *great* food. That became instilled in the minds of his sons. And so, when it came time for his son Hunter to decide what he wanted to do when he grew up, the culinary arts were a logical choice. He had, after all, grown up loving to cook and eat. Because Hunter had been raised on a high standard of what is good and what is delicious, he knows the difference between the two. He sets an incredibly high bar for the food he serves and what it should taste like. And we, Nashville, get to enjoy those amazing dishes made by Hunter Sympson, the Mobile Chef.

The versatility that Hunter Sympson brings to the Mobile Chef is ridiculous. He can literally do anything. But the genre of flavors that he prefers and that form the majority of his menu is what Hunter calls "South by Southwest." Gordon tells me that Hunter's favorite thing is to smoke meats, and he is at the commissary smoking meat almost any day he isn't in the truck at a lunch service or private event, testing different temperatures, meats and spices. His smoked pulled pork sliders won first place in the Best Smoked category at the 2013 Nashville Street Food Awards. He then takes that southern smoked meat component and fuses it with Southwest flavor, either through spices and/or presentation.

Hunter is a Le Cordon Bleu–trained chef. After spending years working in professional kitchens from Hawaii to Sarasota, Florida, and most recently as the executive chef at the Hilton Downtown here in Nashville, Hunter decided it was time to run his own kitchen. He absolutely loves the catering business, and that was his mindset when he started the Mobile Chef. When the food truck scene really began to pick up here in Nashville, Hunter saw the opportunity to expand the vision of the Mobile Chef. And we are so lucky for that expansion.

When you visit his truck, you are given a high-quality, gourmet, from-scratch meal that is really fine dining in casual attire. His food is like Giorgio Armani jeans. They might be jeans, but they are still Armani. There might be a taco or a burrito on the menu at the Mobile Chef, but what's inside is ridiculous gourmet food.

Because Hunter is a chef first, his mindset is always on bringing to the table the freshest ingredients possible. He loves fresh. He loves unprocessed. And the flavors in his food present themselves as such. This is also his mindset when he takes the truck to a lunch service or catering event. The people he has working with him in the mobile kitchen are chefs he has worked with in the past in professional kitchens. He is truly bringing that professional, big-kitchen atmosphere to a smaller scale, and because of that, he is able to present foods with a lot of versatility and dimension. He is able to produce a wide range of foods on the truck because those in his mobile kitchen have the same range. He does not have to retrain everyone every time there is a menu change.

Hunter's was one of the first trucks last summer to bring a lighter side to its menu. He was one of the trendsetters who had a fresh summer salad available. With fresh spinach and a homemade strawberry vinaigrette, it was a filling salad that was still light, refreshing and full of flavor. He also does a version of the southern classic fried okra—fresh from the farm okra that is lightly breaded and deep-fried.

Anything that involves his smoked brisket or his pulled pork, or any of his other smoked meats, is going to be a flavor explosion. The meat is always tender and spiced right. Every single time I have ordered something with his smoked meats, the meat is consistently super tender. It really is delicious.

His first love, though, is catering. And he is building a stellar reputation around the wedding circuit, as well as at private corporate lunches and events. When you view the menu on his website, it's more aimed at catering. His street food menu is based on what he is able to buy fresh that week and what he is inspired to make when he sees the fresh fruit, vegetables and meats available. This catering aspect was the driving force behind the set up of his mobile kitchen, which is a twenty-two-foot trailer with a generator that could power a house in the bed of the truck that pulls the trailer. Because of this, the Mobile Chef can offer some items that other trucks cannot—like fountain soda drinks. Instead of canned pop or twenty-ounce bottles, Hunter has a fountain setup so you can get the pop straight from the draft. And isn't that so much better than a can or bottle?

It's hard for me to talk about any specific item from his truck because his menu is always changing based on the ingredients available to him, the season and his culinary inspirations that particular week. What I can tell you is that you won't be disappointed when you order food from him. I'm calling a visit to his truck a "casual fine dining street food experience." He's really one of the few truck owners who can get away with constantly changing menu choices because of the quality of the food and also because his main focus is catering. Lots of people want to do a little bit of everything, but they fail because they can't do a little bit of everything well. While Hunter's main comfort zone is the South-by-Southwest style, he really does a lot of a little bit of everything well. It takes a chef a long time and experience to be able to achieve this.

I always love running into Hunter and ordering from his truck when I see him out—mainly because he is just a true down-to-earth guy with a ton of fun stories. When I had the opportunity to meet his father, Gordon, I realized that he is so much like his dad—their sensibilities and views on food, their storytelling, their way of introducing things that seem refined and making them approachable (they may or may not have introduced me to caviar) and their ease in getting me to try a pickle slice. So many people try this and so few succeed. (For the record, I liked their pickle, too.)

Let Hunter Sympson and the Mobile Chef take your taste buds on a culinary adventure. To book the Mobile Chef for your corporate lunch or event or wedding, you can visit its website (www.tnmobilechef.com), Facebook page (The-Mobile-Chef) or Twitter feed (@HunterSympson).

The Mobile Chef's Cedar Plank Mustard-Rubbed Salmon with Israeli Couscous and Fire-Roasted Mixed Veggies
(Recipe provided by Hunter Sympson)

Cedar plank
1 side salmon
½ cup spicy mustard
1 red onion, shaved
2 tablespoons capers
3 cups Israeli couscous
4–5 cups chicken broth
1 red pepper
1 yellow pepper
1 yellow squash
1 zucchini
Olive oil, salt and pepper to taste

Preheat oven to 425 degrees. Soak the cedar plank for at least 30 minutes in cold water. Lightly rub salmon with spicy mustard and then layer the shaved red onions and capers on top of the mustard-rubbed salmon. Put the salmon on the cedar plank and grill for 25 minutes.

Layer the Israeli couscous in the bottom of a hotel pan. Heat chicken broth to boiling in a medium-large pot and pour over the couscous. Wrap and let sit for 3 minutes. The couscous is now ready to serve.

Largely dice the peppers, squash and zucchini. Toss in olive oil, salt and pepper to taste. Bake at 425 degrees for 12 minutes.

THE TRUCKS

MOOVERS AND SHAKERS

Back in 2011, Hayden Coleman was a music business and business entrepreneurship student at Belmont University. He and his friends were walking down Belmont Boulevard past a set of shops run by students through the Center for Entrepreneurship. Seeing that a space that had been previously home to a CD shop was now empty, Hayden and his friends started to contemplate what would move in there next. Throwing out ideas, the thought of an old-school ice cream parlor popped up. That area of town really doesn't have anything like that, and the only real hangout around there is Bongo Java, but that gets so crowded and a bit smoky outside the door. The friends were talking about this ice cream parlor idea, thinking it would be a great community hangout for Belmont students.

This brought Hayden back to many fond childhood memories. A Gulf Shore native, Hayden's mom worked at an independent pharmacy that still had an operational soda counter. Every day after school, Hayden would run over to the pharmacy's soda counter with his friends. So the thought of having that in Nashville really got Hayden excited.

About that time, word about the Grilled Cheeserie was beginning to spread like wildfire and inspired many people to look more closely at starting up mobile food concepts. Hayden and a friend were both made aware of a business plan competition hosted by the Center for Entrepreneurship. After much thought, they decided to enter the competition. After hours upon hours of developing the business plan, Hayden and his business partner took second place. Then, after putting together a Kickstarter campaign, they raised enough money to purchase their Moovers and Shakers van. After reworking the plumbing, mechanical wiring and the basic interior of the truck in order to pass their health inspection, finally, in May 2011, Moovers and Shakers hit the streets officially.

One of the things Hayden can't express enough is how amazing the Belmont Center for Entrepreneurship is. He would be taking a class and was able to do his assigned class projects on Moovers and Shakers. It enabled him to learn a lot about the business side of running a food truck as it was happening to him. He was able to have a team of scholastic professionals helping him work through some of the major business issues. And it was part of his collegiate experience and education.

One of the neat things about Moovers and Shakers is its "pun names" for its creations, not to mention the fact that the truck's name is a pun. A good example is the Don't Go Bacon My Heart, a chocolate, peanut butter and bacon milkshake and one of the most popular flavors, which we hope will be a permanent addition to the menu. A favorite of many food truck owners and their employees is the Foreign Exchange Student, which has brown sugar, cinnamon, vanilla extract, jerk seasoning and Sriracha. Hayden loves finding themes for their menus and tying in the flavor names to those themes. The "Back to School" menu features shakes like the Berry

Bruin (Belmont) and the Chocodore (Vanderbilt). It's worth visiting the truck just for the entertainment of seeing the menu board!

Hayden is always challenging himself. Anytime he goes to a restaurant or eats or drinks anything, he is always asking himself, "How can I put this in a milkshake?" (My response, "Like pop rocks?" And if or when that happens, Nashville, you're welcome!) He also does blended floats where he replaces the milk in a milkshake with fountain soda. So while a milkshake can sometimes feel a little heavy, utilizing the fountain soda makes it lighter, and the soda helps quench your thirst more than milk does in a traditional milkshake.

Because Moovers and Shakers is a milkshake food truck, winter is not a season when it would typically do good business, so it does close down for the cold months. It was something that Hayden and his partner anticipated from the onset. They run a business model to operate nine or ten months of the year but have the ability to pay a full twelve months' worth of expenses. One thing that surprised me—and Hayden mentioned that it was a surprise to him as well—is that in late July and August, the humidity and heat here in Nashville are just as bad for business as snow and rain. I've said it before and I'll say it again: Nashvillians are fair-weather fans. While I agree that it sucks to stand in the heat at the height of the summer, I for one will go outside and get a milkshake to help cool me down. And Hayden's shakes are thirst-quenching and delicious.

For this season, Moovers and Shakers is going to stay in the same vehicle where it started in the business, but hopefully, coming in 2015, it will move to a larger, traditional-sized food truck. This season, there are some changes happening to the truck, so be on the lookout for those. I don't want to spoil any surprises, but I will say that the changes will help bring Moovers and Shakers back to Hayden's childhood roots.

While going to school full time and running a food truck business has been difficult to balance, Hayden was able to do both successfully. Starting as a sophomore at Belmont when Moovers and Shakers opened, he was able to grow the business each year despite the fact that he was in school. And now that he has graduated and can fully focus on Moovers and Shakers, there are some bigger and better things that will happen with the truck in 2014 and beyond.

If you are looking for Moovers and Shakers or would like to book it for your private event, visit its website (www.mooversandshakersnashville.com), Facebook page or Twitter feed (@MooversShakers).

Moovers and Shakers Caribbean-Spiced Nut Shake
(Recipe provided by Hayden Coleman)

1 serving = 16 ounces

8 ounces whole milk (for that creamy goodness!)
5–6 scoops of premium vanilla ice cream (depending on desired thickness)
1 cup raw, whole hazelnuts
$1/3$ cup diced walnuts
¼ teaspoon cinnamon
3 pinches of Caribbean jerk seasoning
Vanilla crème syrup

Blend together ingredients for a taste of the islands with a kick! Garnish with 3 or 4 hazelnuts, a dash of diced walnuts, a pinch of cinnamon and a drizzle of vanilla crème syrup on top (optional)

Music City Pie Company

When this book was still an idea, I would have written a completely different story here. But due to a change in circumstances, the story for this truck is of a new truck instead of a truck that is almost a year old. Originally opened in July 2013, the owner grew the truck and its following, even securing a spot inside LP Field to serve his pies at the Titans' NFL games. The original concept was inspired by the owner's visit to Australia, where pies are common street food and served on every corner. After working the truck for the final half of 2013, due to personal circumstances, he decided to see if there was anyone interested in buying the business.

Enter Jenny Clarke and Jason Cook. They were all set to fly to Portland to look at and hopefully purchase a truck for their concept and then bring the truck back to Nashville. As fate would have it, the night before their trip, they saw an ad for Music City Pie Company on a website. They called and spoke with the former owner, canceled their flights to Portland and are now the proud new owners of Music City Pie Company. After working through a transition period, learning the recipes and getting more familiar with the truck, Jenny and Jason officially opened in January 2014. The recipes for the menu items that were already favorites remain the same. Going forward, the new menu items will now be Jason's originals.

Jason has an extensive background in commercial kitchens. From Minneapolis to Los Angeles, he has worked with and learned from some amazing chefs. With most of the pies and their fillings being made from scratch, Jason arrives at the commissary very early each day. Let's just say it's still dark outside, and the rest of us in Nashville haven't even thought about opening our eyes—and won't for a number of hours.

Jenny's background is in hospitality. She is handling growing the catering side of the business, dealing with the bookings and locations and working the social media accounts. Honestly, this is a brilliant partnership. Let the chef do what he does best—cook. Let the businessperson handle everything else.

Music City Pie Company has a few exciting things happening in 2014. Not only does it have that spot at LP Field, but it is coordinating with a few local coffee shops to help expand their food offerings by featuring Music City Pie Company Pies. It is also looking into bringing the take-and-bake pie to its menu.

The truck serves five-inch pies. While at first glance they might look small, the fillings are pretty substantial. My first experience was last summer when I ordered the Cajun Pie. I exchanged glances with my boyfriend, thinking it was really small. However, by the time I finished my pie, I was actually comfortable. I wasn't stuffed, but I definitely was not hungry. And the savory pie filling was done *very* well.

From the Drunk Lil' Piggy Pie to the traditional Chicken (pot) Pie to the Cajun Pie, the savory pies are perfect to sate an appetite and large enough to pack a full punch of

flavor. The Drunk Lil' Piggy Pie is full of pulled pork shoulder with a bacon and white bean gravy, mixed veggies and a tomato whiskey sauce. There is also Zippy's Meatball pie, full of Italian-style meatballs, marinara and mozzarella cheese—fuhgeddaboutit and just order it already!

As for the traditional sweet pies, Music City Pie Company almost always has a custard pie of some sort on board and has started to do mini chess pies as well. Its fruit pies are seasonal and based on what is in season and fresh. So make sure to check the menu board to see what the featured sweet pies are. Last summer, I had the peach and bacon pie, and it was phenomenal!

As for their original truck concept, just in case Jason and Jenny decide to open a second truck, I'll let them surprise you. Jenny let me know what it was and also made it known that Music City Pie Company will always be Music City Pie Company. They are aiming to take Music City Pie Company to bigger and better things. Jason is constantly creating pie fillings (both savory and sweet) that he looks forward to bringing to his customers. And who doesn't love pie? It's a very American thing.

One of the things I truly love about Music City Pie Company and Jenny and Jason is this: Music City Pie Company was a great concept and was putting out good pies. Had Jenny and Jason not bought the business, this would have most likely been another one for the food truck graveyard. And that's a sad thing because it was (and is) a great concept with great food. And if they had opened their own truck, Jenny and Jason would be doing the normal new food truck owner song and dance and coming up against a lot of hurdles that put a lot of young food trucks out of business. Here, they can stay true to the heart of what they wanted to do with their original concept of creating from-scratch gourmet food and owning and operating a food truck in Nashville, but without some of the headaches of starting completely from nothing.

Even though Music City Pie Company itself isn't new, Jenny and Jason still have the distinction of being new food truck owners. They've still faced some challenges, especially when it comes to the operation of the physical food truck. Jenny told me what is now a cute story but was probably stress inducing at the time about one of their first nights on the truck when the lights inside the truck wouldn't work (fyi, they just needed to fill up with gas). So instead of adding to the current saturation of the food truck market with a new concept and a new truck, we get to welcome two new food truck owners while keeping one of our Nashville favorites on the streets.

To check out and keep up with Music City Pie Company, visit its Facebook page or Twitter feed (@MusicCityPieCo).

Broken Heart Chick Pie

1 tablespoon olive oil

1 tablespoon butter

4–6 skinless, boneless organic chicken breasts (seasoned to your liking with salt, pepper, oil and garlic powder), diced

1 16-ounce can artichoke hearts, drained, quartered and then cut into small halves (reserve the drained liquid)

3 onions, diced

1½ cups fresh mushrooms, sliced

½ cup white wine

1 tablespoon capers

5 ounces cream cheese

1 homemade or frozen nine-inch pie or pastry shell

$1/3$ cup Asiago cheese, shredded (plus more for additional topping after the pie has baked)

Preheat oven to 400 degrees.

Heat oil and butter in a large skillet over medium heat. Brown diced and seasoned chicken for 5 to 7 minutes per side. Remove from skillet and set aside.

Place artichoke hearts, onions and mushrooms in a skillet and sauté until mushrooms are brown and tender. Return chicken to the skillet and pour in reserved artichoke liquid and wine. Reduce heat to low and simmer for about 10 to 15 minutes or until chicken is no longer pink and juices run clear.

Stir in capers and simmer for another 5 minutes. Remove from heat.

Mix all together with cream cheese. Let simmer for 5 to 8 minutes, stirring until the cream cheese is melted. Turn off the heat and let the filling rest, then fill the pie shell with the filling. Add the Asiago cheese, then place dough on top and crimp to hold in place.

Bake for 15 to 20 minutes. Once out of the oven, if desired, add some additional shredded Asiago cheese on top.

Retro Sno

The more than ninety minutes that I got to sit down and chat with Elizabeth Nunnally and Morgan Williamson at their commissary were some of the most enjoyable time I've ever had. Honestly, they are two of the sweetest people in the food truck scene, so it helps that they are running one of the best sweet trucks out there. I think if Retro Sno had a theme song that played while they drove up to a location, it would be Pharrell Williams's "Happy." They just have a good vibe all around, and they are serving up childhood memories all over middle Tennessee.

Elizabeth and Morgan are best friends. Elizabeth had been running a summer camp and was looking to hire a replacement, as she was moving to Nashville. Enter Morgan. We'll bypass a bit to say that Morgan did not love running the summer camp the way Elizabeth loved it. But the point of this is that they met, discovered that they worked well together and become fast friends. After Morgan and her husband moved to Nashville, Elizabeth and Morgan found themselves talking one day. Morgan mentioned her obsession with Sno Balls. This goes back to Morgan's high school years in Texas. There was a little Sno Ball shack outside her high school, and she would literally have a Sno Ball every single day. Both Morgan and Elizabeth were looking forward to the next phase of their lives, and they really started to talk about bringing the Sno Ball concept to Nashville. After doing months of research through the end of 2011 and then finally purchasing their truck (lovingly named Razz) in February 2012, Retro Sno was born!

Sno Balls originated in New Orleans, so Elizabeth and Morgan say that Retro Sno is a New Orleans–style Sno Ball. While a Sno Ball is similar in concept to a Sno Cone, the difference lies in the process of shaving versus crushing the ice. The exciting thing that Elizabeth mentioned was that Retro Sno was going to start making its own blocks of ice in 2014. Not only will this help to keep costs down, but the owners will also have more control over every ingredient and step of the process that goes into the creation of their Sno Balls.

Coming up with new flavors for Sno Balls in my head is like a childhood dream come true. Elizabeth and Morgan both laughed when I mentioned this. Depending on what flavors, and how many, are being tested, it can add up to a lot of sugar intake. Elizabeth goes into a sugar coma, and Morgan begins bouncing off the walls. This is a good representation of their different personalities. While I will say that they are very similar minded in how they experience things and what they enjoy, they have drastically different personalities. Elizabeth is more laidback and reserved—quiet almost—but always has a smile on her face. Morgan is very outgoing and boisterous—and also always has a smile on her face. Their dynamic works very well. I felt like I had known them my whole life. They just had a way of putting me at ease and making me feel immediately like family. And when you visit the truck, you get the exact same experience. Every time someone, big or small, comes to their window, it truly makes them gleeful. The fact that someone chooses to come to their truck and eat their product makes them feel so humbled and excited. When they see someone's face light up after taking a bite of their Sno Ball, their days are literally made. So basically, their days are made with each and every Sno Ball that goes out the window.

While they have the classic grape and cherry—what I call everyday flavors—they also have some creations that are pretty awesome for a Sno Ball. It transforms the Sno Ball from flavored ice into a sweet dessert experience. From German Chocolate Cake to Raspberry Wedding Cake to the kid favorite, Rainbow, and my favorite, Chai, the Sno Balls are sizeable and beautifully garnished. Oh, and they taste great!

In 2013, they started to create some Sno Ball versions that had ice cream underneath the Sno Ball. This adds another dimension to the whole Sno Ball experience, although it is a little messier. OK, here's the thing about Sno Balls and why we loved them as kids: they are tasty and just a little bit messy. Even though you eat these with a spoon (or not), if you don't come away with a little stickiness on your fingertips or running down your hands and arms, you're eating them wrong.

Again, as Retro Sno is a sweet truck centered on something cold, Elizabeth and Morgan shut down in the winter. That was part of their business model, although they do schedule catering events and weddings throughout all twelve months of the year. This allows Elizabeth and Morgan the winter months to pursue some of their side projects. Morgan, for example, is a talented artist and is very crafty. She is the driving force behind everything visual on the truck, and in the off-season, she focuses on her art and creates handmade pottery. With the truck open from only the spring through the fall, the year 2013 was a bit of a difficult one for Retro Sno, as the truck had a plethora of work done. And it seemed as though once they discovered one problem and fixed that, a new problem would pop up. So Retro Sno was out of commission from about July 2013 through the end of the fall.

There is something that Retro Sno started doing that many of the trucks are now doing: merchandising. Retro Sno was one of the first, if not *the* first, trucks to start selling T-shirts. Elizabeth and Morgan even held a contest last season via social media for a new T-shirt design. While getting away from the traditional Sno Ball Styrofoam bowl was more of a challenge than they thought it was going to be, they were also one of the first to use eco-conscious bowls and utensils on their truck.

After a disappointing 2013 with truck issues, they are back in 2014 with a vengeance. Some exciting things are coming, and we are very excited for them. We also cannot wait for their return to the Nashville Street Food Awards. They won the People's Choice in 2012 and also placed second in the Best Drink category with their Chai Ice (there's a reason it's my favorite!). And this was by far both

Elizabeth and Morgan's favorite day on the truck. Having all the trucks alongside them and the excitement of the nearly five thousand people in attendance that day is something they look to forward to when the 2014 Nashville Street Food Awards take place this fall.

Morgan just wants Nashville to love Sno Balls as much as she loves them. To find the Retro Sno truck or book it for a private event, you can check out its website (www. Retro Snotruck.com), Facebook page or Twitter feed (@Retro Sno).

RIFFS FINE STREET FOOD

Riffs Fine Street Food was in that first group of food trucks that emerged in 2011 after the Grilled Cheeserie gained attention and paved the way. The story goes that the owners met while doing some relief work after the Great Flood of 2010. They decided to come together and create something spectacular.

A transplant from Barbados and a trained chef, Carlos spent the decade prior to joining Riffs as a chef at the Loews Vanderbilt Hotel. He brought Caribbean flair and some serious culinary panache to the duo, as well as some major catering and big event experience.

Having spent the majority of his life in professional kitchens, but also having a good bit of business experience, BJ Lofback had a penchant for Asian fusion food but also just really loves food in general. And like so many other food truck proprietors, he gravitated toward the food truck idea when he need a change in his life. BJ tells a story of lying in bed and realizing he wanted to run a food truck. Freaking out his wife in the middle of the night by saying, "I'm going to own a food truck," and shortly thereafter putting his savings into this venture, he had no choice but to find some way to make this work. And work it definitely has.

The meeting of Carlos and BJ seemed to be kismet, and Riffs was off and running. BJ's business background mixed with the deliciously crafted fare of both Carlos and BJ really played a big roll in helping to create buzz for the truck at the beginning. Theirs was, after all, one of the original group of trucks and is now one of the most well-known and recognizable trucks with an extremely loyal fan base.

Riffs was also one of the first trucks to be featured on the Cooking Channel's *Eat Street*. Carlos's specialty family recipe cod balls are probably one of my favorite things I've ever had from Riffs. And unfortunately, they had these on the truck only once at the 2012 Nashville Street Food Awards. Close your eyes. Imagine a really good hushpuppy. Now multiply "really good" by "ridiculous" and add in some cod, and it probably still won't equal how delicious they are.

One of the other stellar onetime items that Riffs has served was a Taiwanese-style bao with oxtail at the inaugural Franklin Food Fight in 2012. Steamed bun deliciousness is what that was! At another of the Food Fight Events, BJ created a BLT utilizing Porter Road Butcher bacon pâté. I mean, bacon pâté—why not? On another Friday evening down on First Avenue in downtown Nashville on National Hot Dog Day, BJ was making foot-long hot dog extravaganzas. There was the Angry Dog topped with kimchi and Sriracha mayo. There was also the Guido Dog, which was topped with grilled sausage, onion and peppers and then finished with Cheese Whiz.

BJ loves the ability to have a different menu every day. He appreciates being able to always utilize the freshest of ingredients, and changing the menu daily means he will never get bored. The only downside is that I do think about those hot dogs and the cod

balls from time to time, and I know they don't make regular appearances on the menu (or even a once-a-year appearances). There are so many great things that I have eaten from the truck that I have never been able to have again. And that makes me a little sad. I appreciate the freedom that they strive for with their menu, and I do understand it, but sometimes rotating in popular items isn't a bad thing (hint, hint).

Riffs is one of the few trucks that has really succeeded in the expansion phase of its business. By 2013, Riffs Fine Street Food expanded to include a catering side of the business. It was getting so popular that the catering requests were overwhelming, and there was no way the truck could be out serving the public and also catering an event. So BJ and Carlos reorganized, with BJ focusing on the food truck operations and Carlos focusing on the catering. With this separation of focus, they now could be in two places at the same time.

The other major expansion was the addition of a brick-and-mortar café in the Donelson area of town, out near the airport. BJ is brilliantly building a team of extremely talented individuals to run the kitchen at the café, as well as the truck; for example, he brought on board Sean Brashears, former owner of Wrapper's Delight food truck. It was recently announced that Riffs is adding a second food truck to now have a small fleet. This second truck will focus on the sweet side of life as Riffs Fine Sweet Foods. BJ hopes to have this truck operational by the summer of 2014. There are other expansion ideas that he has in the pipeline, and they are all good things for Riffs and Nashville.

Riffs is one of the premier examples of what can happen when you have a business savvy mind, a brilliantly talented chef and a stellar business model. Having put some focus in getting the café up and running, BJ is now ready to get the Riffs Fine Street Foods truck back on the streets on a regular basis and bring all that good food to his loyal fan base. While in the beginning there were a lot of onetime items on the menu, Riffs tries to do that less and less these days. It does have some items that make regular appearances, like the über popular Korean Fried Chicken Wings. In 2012 and 2013, Riffs took home the Best of the Best at the Nashville Street Food Awards. It placed or won in nearly every category in both years. Events like the Nashville Street Food Awards really bring out the creativity of the team at Riffs Fine Street Foods. But there's also the added pressure year after year to continue that quality and creativity. I'm always interested to see what items they will enter each year, and I can't wait to see what they unveil at the 2014 Nashville Street Food Awards.

If you are interested in a catering or private event, you can check out Riffs website (www.riffscatering.com), Facebook page (Riffs Catering) page or Twitter feed (@RiffsCatering).

To keep up with the truck and locations, visit the truck's website (www.riffstruck.com), Facebook page (Riffs Fine Street Food) or Twitter feed (@riffstruck).

To see the hours of operation for the Riffs Café at Highland Ridge in Donelson, check out its Facebook page (Riffs Café).

Riffs Fine Street Food Kimchi-Fried Rice
(Recipe provided by BJ Lofback)

Preparation time: 20 minutes / Serves 4

2–3 strips thick-cut bacon, cut in lardons
1 egg, beaten
2 tablespoons vegetable oil
4 cups steamed rice (cold, preferably day-old rice)
2 cups roughly chopped kimchi (older kimchi is best)
1 tablespoon Gochujang (Korean red pepper paste)
1 small bunch green onions, chopped (save ½ for garnish)
¼ cup kimchi juice (from the jar of kimchi)
2 tablespoon light soy sauce
1 tablespoon sesame oil
4–6 turns fresh black pepper

In a cast-iron pan over medium heat, begin cooking the bacon.

In a separate bowl, add egg and oil to cold rice. Using gloved hands or a rice paddle, break up the rice until each grain is coated with the egg-oil mixture and no large clumps of rice remain.

When bacon begins to brown, drain some grease from pan but leave enough to cover the bottom. Add the kimchi and cook for another 3 minutes. Add the Gochujang and stir until it incorporates into the kimchi. In the final minute of cooking, add ½ of the green onions and continue to cook. In all, kimchi cooking time is approximately 6 or 7 minutes.

Add rice and stir into kimchi mixture. If rice starts to stick, add a little bit of oil and keep stirring. Add kimchi juice and then soy sauce to taste. Allow rice to sit undisturbed for a few minutes and let the rice on the bottom get crispy.

Just as you remove from heat, drizzle with sesame oil and black pepper. Serve with over-easy fried eggs and garnish with remaining green onion. Adjust the amount of Gochujang for your spice preference. This is excellent with grilled pork or chicken.

THE ROLLING FEAST

Chef Tom Mead has spent most of his time working in a kitchen, which is a bit funny because he said that growing up, he really did not like food. But after getting one of his first jobs at a restaurant, starting low on the totem pole and then working his way up, as so many truck owners and chefs have, he started to see what was possible with food and flavors. And his work in the culinary field began to grow after that. A graduate of the California Culinary Academy in the Bay Area, Tom spent years honing his art and gaining much-earned acclaim. After years working in several fine dining and upscale eateries from Arizona to the East Coast, Tom and his wife (also a California Culinary Academy graduate) finally settled here in Nashville with their young family. And we are extremely lucky to have them.

When I sat down with Tom, I asked him about his southwestern influence. Obviously, his years in Arizona were a major factor, but he really just loves flavorful foods and spices. The southwestern style really lends itself to the use of a lot of spices and the creation of exquisite flavors. And one of his major goals is to bring flavor to our city's streets. Actually, his range for cooking is quite broad. While he was in Arizona, he worked at fine dining establishments that focused on European cuisine and French-inspired southwestern cuisine.

As he was thinking about the concept for his truck, there were not a lot of southwestern-style trucks in the city, if any. But while his menu currently focuses on the southwestern style, he has left himself open to showing Nashville a variety of flavors, and he is gaining a number of loyal fans, many within the food truck community itself. I heard about the Rolling Feast before I had the opportunity to try his truck—before I had ever seen his truck, in fact. Ryan from the Waffle Boss was one of the first to mention the Rolling Feast. He could not say enough nice things about Tom and his food. And I've heard a few other food truck owners say the same things. My interest was piqued. So

finally, last summer at a Friday night food truck frenzy, we finally got to visit his truck. Jim is a huge carnitas fan, so when he saw Green Chile Carnitas on the menu, he was pretty excited and a bit nervous. (I say nervous only because if the carnitas didn't live up to his standard, it would be game over for Jim and the Rolling Feast. Jim's a little stricter than I am on how many tries he'll give a truck before benching it.) Jim took one bite, and I knew immediately that what everyone was saying was true: Tom was legit. I was barely able to beg a few bites of the carnitas—they were so good, Jim didn't want to share!

I know I say this next bit a lot, but to me it is what separates the man trucks from the boy trucks, the good from the bad. If done well, it can vault you into the top tier of food trucks versus being just an average Joe. I'm talking about having the philosophy of preparing your food from scratch. Tom bakes his own hot dog buns for his Sonoran Dog. And he bakes them *on the truck*. That's ridiculous, right? He fries the tortilla chips for his Chicken Nachos and his Spicy Chicken Tortilla Soup. Fresh. From scratch. Unprocessed. It really makes a world of difference in bettering the flavor of the food.

OK, now I need to tell you about his Sonoran Dog. Tom charges only four dollars for this, and it is a *steal*. The Sonoran Dog is a bacon-wrapped, all-beef hot dog in a fresh bun that has been baked on the truck topped with pinto beans, salsa verde, tomato, onions, mustard and mayo. "Legitimately Awesome Dog" is more like it. Who doesn't love a good hot dog wrapped in bacon? The addition of the pinto beans might seem strange written on a menu board, but it makes so much sense when you eat it. And the homemade, baked-on-the-truck bun is what makes this truly stand out above nearly every other hot dog being served.

Tom's Spicy Chicken Tortilla Soup was something he added around the fall when the weather got cooler. I really love this soup. I've told Tom he needs to start selling it in pints and quarts so I can bring it home. And lucky for us, Tom provided the recipe for this book. It isn't just some bland broth with chicken and veggies thrown in. Oh no! This soup has dynamite flavor and is the perfect level of spicy. It was spicier than I anticipated, but in a good way. The chicken is tender. And when you dig your spoon all the way to the bottom of the bowl, you get a big hunk of melted cheese, avocado, a little bit of chicken and broth—it is one of the best spoonfuls! Add in the crunch from his truck-fried tortilla chips, and it's a serious flavor explosion. But even with the small amount of cheese, this soup is not heavy or unhealthy. You can eat it without feeling any guilt whatsoever.

My next favorite item from his truck—and I will order this even if I'm getting the soup—is Tom's Spinach Salad. Even at nine dollars, this salad is a steal. Topped with spiced candied pecans, which I hoard until the end and eat as my reward for eating a salad, the bed of baby spinach is also covered in grilled chicken, shaved Vermont cheddar and red onions and then tossed in a homemade citrus vinaigrette. The first time I had this salad, there were also some pear slices, and the vinaigrette was pear (because, clearly, pears were in season). This salad is versatile in that it lends itself to be adjusted based on what fruits are in season. This seems like a simple dish, but the addition of the shaved Vermont cheddar

and the spiced candied pecans make it a spectacular salad. And Tom makes a mean citrus vinaigrette! It has sweetness and a bit of a tang that play so well with the crispness of the red onion and the sharpness of the cheddar.

At a recent Musician's Corner event, which was also one of the first times we visited the Rolling Feast, we had the Prosciutto, Roasted Tomato and Goat Cheese Quesadilla. A perfect handheld food, this was one of our favorite items from that day of eating from several trucks. The saltiness from the prosciutto was cut by the creaminess of the goat cheese and roasted tomato. And it is one of the largest quesadillas I've ever been served. Whereas normally people take a large flour tortilla and fold it in half, this was a large flour tortilla, with filling, topped with another large flour tortilla. It was literally the same size as the large dinner-sized paper plate it was served on. It was a good thing Jim and I were splitting it!

When Tom does dessert, do not pass it up—even if you have to save it to eat later. At the 2013 Nashville Street Food Awards, Tom created a Pumpkin Cheesecake that was mind blowing. I quickly ate it

up before Jim arrived because I didn't want to share. When I went back up to order another piece for Jim, Tom had sold out. It was a sad moment for me, but I'm always happy to hear when my favorite trucks sell out. Showing a bit of his versatility and international flair, Tom placed second in the Best Yazoo category at the Nashville Street Food Awards with his mussels cooked in Yazoo beer. There was obviously more to the dish than that, and he had a few leftovers that he shared with us. I love mussels, and these were well done—in a food truck! Maybe one day we can talk him into putting them on the menu. He also placed third in the Best Vegetarian category with his Chilaquiles. (I'm still wondering how that Pumpkin Cheesecake didn't place because it really was spectacular.)

I guarantee that the food you order from Tom and the Rolling Feast will be full of flavor because that is what he loves. I guarantee that the food will be fresh and from scratch and that a good bit of it was made on the truck. I guarantee that Tom will appreciate any and all feedback you have. He said that when he has the time on the truck, he loves chatting with his customers, finding out how they discovered his truck and what they thought of the food. And sometimes his very sweet mother is with him on the truck. She has such a warm and welcoming smile. And at big events, you might catch Tom putting the kids to work pouring the lemonade or helping to take the orders.

The Rolling Feast is rolling to an area near you every day. And Tom deserves the opportunity to earn your repeat business. To follow his truck's movements and book your private event or catering, you can check out the truck's website (www. therollingfeast.com), Facebook page or Twitter feed (@therollingfeast).

The Rolling Feast's Spicy Chicken Tortilla Soup
(Recipe provided by Tom Mead)

Serves 8

2 tablespoons vegetable oil
1 small onion, diced
2 tablespoons garlic
2 quarts chicken stock
1 cup roasted tomatoes or peeled San Marzano tomatoes
1 tablespoon cumin
1 teaspoon dried oregano
1 teaspoon ground coriander
1 teaspoon red pepper flakes
1 pound chicken breasts
2 limes, for juice and wedges
¼ bunch cilantro
4 small tomatoes, diced
2 avocados
4 cups shredded Jack cheese
Salt to taste
Fried tortilla strips

In a large saucepan, heat the vegetable oil. Add the onions and cook for 2 minutes. Once the onions have softened, add the garlic and cook for another minute. Pour the chicken stock, tomatoes, cumin, oregano, coriander and red pepper flakes into the pot and bring to a boil. Once at a boil, lower the heat to a simmer and add the chicken breasts. Cook the chicken for 20 to 25 minutes. Once chicken is cooked, remove from the pot. When cool enough to handle, shred it and set it aside. Add lime juice and fresh cilantro to the pot. In a serving bowl, add a mound of shredded chicken, fresh tomatoes, avocado, cheese, cilantro and lime juice. Salt to taste. Ladle soup into bowls and top with a lime wedge and fried tortilla strips.

Slow Hand Coffee Company

Starting in 2013, coffee nerd and java extraordinaire Nick Guidry has been utilizing a time-consuming process called cold brewing, which produces a naturally sweeter taste with lower acidity, to make his coffee. This creates a higher-quality, better-tasting coffee. To clarify, cold brewing is not making iced coffee; it is a process used to make regular coffee. For iced coffee, it must be poured over ice.

Hating the corporate life, Nick moved to head up the marketing for a coffee roaster in Raleigh, North Carolina. After a few years of getting his java toes wet, he graduated to the big leagues to work for a major coffee corporation, where he oversaw nearly three hundred cafés and traveled all across the United States. After the wear and tear of being a road warrior finally took its toll, Nick decided he wanted his own coffee bistro café where he could do things his way. Originally having a brick-and-mortar concept in mind, it soon became clear that the banks were not going to make it easy for him to start a business in the food and beverage industry. So after reevaluating his concept, he realized it could succeed as a food truck.

Finding a name for the company was a challenge for Nick. Every name he thought of was already registered. Finally, a good friend suggested the Slow Hand. At the time, Nick still thought his concept would be a brick and mortar. Slow Hand was meant to encompass everything handcrafted, and that still applied as the transition from brick and mortar to food truck occurred. Bucking from the traditional wrap, the Slow Hand truck was hand painted by a craftsman, and Nick crafted the interior of the truck himself. And let's not forget that the coffee is handcrafted, and the hot sandwiches and pastries served are all handcrafted too.

While throughout 2013, Nick did offer hot sandwiches and some pastries, in 2014, Slow Hand Coffee Company introduced its newest addition: pastry chef Audra Dykes. Audra had grown up loving baking and the art of pastry making, having spent so much time with her mom and grandmother baking creations in their kitchens. The only jobs she has ever had have been in the food service industry. So it was natural that she entered culinary school. She was not really a fan of culinary school, and it was not until a demonstration at the school by Jacques Torres (aka Mr. Chocolate), one of the most recognized pastry chefs of our time, that she realized she was just in the wrong culinary program. So she moved to New York and entered the French Culinary Institute's Pastry School, where she became a pastry chef. After working at several establishments around Nashville, including Bound'ry and Coffee, Lunch, she is now the pastry chef for Slow Hand Coffee Company, bringing her grownup interpretations of childhood favorite pastries and snacks to the masses.

Growing up (and sometimes even now), I couldn't help purchasing a box of those individually wrapped sweet treats from Little Debbie's and Hostess—those oatmeal crème pies, Star Crunch and Swiss cake rolls; those boxes you could eat the contents of in one sitting. Well, Audra takes those concepts and makes grownup versions. Her oatmeal crème pies are enormous. The cookies are baked to perfection, with a little crispiness around the edges and then getting softer and cakier as you approach the middle. The icing in the center is so much better than those packaged versions. You take one bite, and you know you will never again be able to have a prepackaged oatmeal crème pie again. To get a cookie that size to be so perfectly baked is truly a special talent. Her version of the Star Crunch is truly inspired. If you think you know a Rice Krispie treat dipped in chocolate, let me tell you right now: you know nothing. When I bought this the first time, I was like, "I know what a Star Crunch is. I could make that at home. It's nothing special." And then I bit into Audra's version. There was the most wonderful caramel gooeyness mixed with the crunch from the rice cereal and then the dark chocolate that melts the minute it hits your mouth. I was glad that she makes such sizeable portions, as I was really able to savor the flavors. Then there is the Swiss cake roll. I literally just sighed at thought of her moist chocolate roulade covered in perfectly tempered dark chocolate. The neat twist? Little bits of sea salt are sprinkled on top. The salt adds that little bit of sophistication and brings a whole new flavor to an old favorite. Don't just order one of her treats. Order one to eat immediately, and then order one to eat after that. This will prevent you having to get back in line to order the inevitable second pastry. Trust me, you'll want it.

Back to the coffee. Nick has an array of homemade syrups on the truck and can do all the upscale favorites. While the name of the truck is Slow Hand, it doesn't mean he is slow at preparing your coffee. He makes coffee just as quickly as any other coffee joint, major chain or local café that serves specialized handcrafted coffee. One of the things I really enjoy about his coffee is that it lacks that bitter taste that turns so many people away from drinking coffee. Jim is not a coffee drinker. At all. And yet, after having a sip of my coffee from the truck, he ordered his own. And drank the entire cup. I'm normally a person who, when it comes to coffee, goes all Beastie Boys: "I like my sugar with coffee and cream." But Nick has a vanilla iced coffee on his menu. I ordered it without any sugar and cream, just the handcrafted vanilla syrup. I couldn't have imagined adding any cream or sugar to that. It was actually perfect straight up with just the vanilla syrup. Again, because the coffee is cold brewed, there is a naturally sweeter taste to it without any additives. And if you add one of Audra's pastries, your sweet tooth will be more than satisfied.

Coffee and pastries have long been partners in crime, and Slow Hand Coffee Company is a prime example of how well the two complement each other. And it's not just coffee and pastries but handcrafted coffee and truly inspired pastries. In 2014, Slow Hand built in a lunch menu and has really been successful, quietly gaining a strong following of its lunchtime offerings. The Satchmo is an oven-roasted brisket sandwich, and the Rio Grande is a green chile mac 'n' cheese topped with fried chicken skin cracklings. And yes, fried chicken skin cracklings are better than bacon bits. They're going to be the new trend—I'm calling it!

In the summer, you can look forward to the return (at least I hope) of the Slow Hand Jalapeño Lemonade. The lemonade is thirst quenching and refreshing, and you get the flavor of the jalapeño without the heat. You aren't just getting another watered-down lemonade but one with flavor. Jalapeño and lemonade were meant to go together.

As with most trucks, there are long-term plans for growth, but for 2014, Nick and Audra want to focus on continuing their momentum and growing their menu to bring you even more amazing coffee creations and pastries. Something tells me we haven't even scratched the surface of what they have in store for us.

To follow the truck or to book it at your property or your private event, visit its website (www.slowhandcoffee.com), Facebook page or Twitter feed (@SlowHandCoffee).

Slow Hand Coffee Company's Sipping Chocolate
(Recipe provided by Nick Guidry)

Makes 4 servings

$1/3$ cup unsweetened cocoa powder
¾ cup white sugar
1 pinch salt
$1/3$ cup water
3½ cups milk
1 teaspoon vanilla extract
1½ cups half & half

Mix dry ingredients in a bowl. Add water to a large saucepan and bring to a boil. Add dry ingredients to the boiling water and then bring down to a simmer for 2 to 3 minutes. Add milk and heat to just before a boil. Remove from heat and add vanilla extract and half & half.

SMOKE ET AL

Shane Autrey is one of the originals of the Nashville food truck scene. He has one of the most storied culinary backgrounds I've ever had the pleasure of hearing about. And he is one amazingly talented barbecue guy. That's a technical term: barbecue guy. Shane is part of a competitive barbecue team: Pig Nation BBQ. The team has been in the competitive arena for quite a while now, and to help make certain aspects of competing easier (setup and cleanup), Shane had the idea of a food truck. So what started as an idea for a competitive barbecue vehicle became one of Nashville's favorite and most popular trucks.

When Smoke Et Al first started, Shane was a busy guy calling the office parks and looking for places to park and set up the truck. He was hustling trying to find locations for lunch service. Nowadays, Shane is so overwhelmed with private event and catering requests that he has to force himself to set aside a few days every week so he can set up for lunch service, and he has his pick of sweet spots. When I was talking with Shane, he said he receives so many catering requests that he wouldn't have to be a food truck

if he didn't want to be anymore. The thing is, he loves bringing his barbecue and his ridiculous gourmet food to the streets of Nashville. So he continues to make serving the public a priority. (As a note, it's always best to get any catering or private request in *months* in advance. Smoke Et Al is probably the most popular food truck on the wedding circuit. And also keep in mind that the Memphis in May BBQ competition keeps him busy for a few weeks in the spring!)

Before you start to compare Smoke Et Al to roadside barbecue stands, remember that most of the guys running the roadside stands are guys who just like to barbecue, and perhaps they've had a lot of people tell them they make great barbecue. And it very well may be good barbecue, but when you order anything else from them, it comes out of a plastic tub that they

bought from a wholesale club. And if you ask them where their meat came from, if the answer isn't the wholesale club, I guarantee you it will be a chain grocery store.

Shane Autrey is one of the most talented chefs in Nashville who does not have a brick and mortar, and his culinary journey makes for a great story—one that may or may not include his getting into a bit of a spat with a gentleman by the name of Eric Rapier. He has worked with the who's who of the who's who in the culinary world. He dropped a lot of names, and while I admit that I knew some, I'm not quite the culinary chef junkie I probably should be. Suffice it to say, barbecue guy's got mad skills. So when you order a side dish, it has been made from scratch. It is not being scooped out of a processed plastic tub. Shane will know the local farm that raised the animals, grew the produce and provided the dairy products. He will know the processes used to process the meat. And because of that, he has better-quality meat to serve.

Because of his skill level, you can be a vegetarian or a vegan and walk up to his truck and ask him if there is anything not on the menu that he could whip up to serve

you. And yes, it might seem crazy for a vegan to walk up to a barbecue truck, but it happens. And you know what? He looks at what's on the truck and creates a dish that many times becomes a rotating item on his menu. Because the truck was originally fit for barbecue competitions, Shane has a full commercial kitchen inside. He does *all* his prep on the truck (with the exception of smoking the meat, although the smoker is sometimes attached to the back of the truck). While most other trucks complete their prep at a commissary, Shane and his brilliant team do all of it on the truck. It still boggles my mind.

Smoke Et Al was one of the first trucks to get national attention from the Cooking Channel's *Eat Street* program. And deservedly so! The thing I loved about watching Smoke Et Al on the show is that the items Shane made during the episode are things I've eaten from the truck. They were not specialty items that were on the truck for that one day or for one week a year. They are so good that they should be specialty items, but he serves them everyday.

When the meat is smoking, there is someone manning that smoker at all times. Unlike many barbecue restaurants that, once they become brick and mortar, end up using pellets or an electric smoker (or maybe that's the same thing and I just don't know), Shane has stayed the course using a wood-fire smoker. And because of that, the smoker is manned at all times to ensure that the temperature on the smoker is what it should be.

The Smoke Et Al team takes extreme time and care in everything it makes, and it comes through in the food. I suggest trying the Fiddler's Biscuits. These were created as a specialty item when the Travel Channel's *Hotel Impossible* came to the Fiddler Inn. Shane makes a sage biscuit and then tops that with some of his amazing smoked chicken. He then drizzles honey from a local bee farm over the top and garnishes with some green onions. Pair that with some of his pickled fried okra or my favorite side, his Guaca'roni Salad, and you have one of the best barbecue meals ever. From his Wedge Oak Farm Pork Belly BLT Tacos to his Memphis-Style Hot Wings to his Pickled Fried Okra and Yazoo Mac and Cheese, there is no way you can walk away from this truck without feeling uncomfortably full and 100 percent sated.

While it might seem that barbecue places are a dime a dozen these days, and that may be true, Smoke Et Al should not and cannot be included in that grouping. While there is smoked chicken, brisket and pork on the menu, it's not just pulled chicken slapped between a grocery store bun and topped with some processed prepackaged coleslaw. It's smoked chicken on a sage bun with some drizzled honey. It's not just fanned-out slices of brisket on a plate with some collard greens and mac 'n' cheese (not that there is anything wrong with that); Shane serves you brisket with feta cheese and Kalamata olives with some tzatziki in a soft taco. And it's not just pork. It is never *just* pork. It is pork belly with bacon, lettuce and tomato salsa. He even elevates the mac 'n' cheese component by adding Yazoo beer to the recipe. While some of the major local barbecue franchises in town aren't using prepackaged ingredients, they are serving barbecue as barbecue. And that is perfectly perfect. But Smoke Et Al is elevated above that level. And that's why I say it can't be compared to any barbecue place you can think of. Barbecue might be the base of the every dish, but each dish is so much more than just the barbecue. Smoke Et Al's slogan says just that: "A boutique, smokin' food truck that goes beyond just BBQ."

That being said, Smoke Et Al will absolutely satisfy your craving if you are looking for just barbecue.

I don't get to visit the Smoke Et Al truck as much as I would like, and now I know that a big reason for that are the private events it is constantly catering. Most trucks strive to have that level of requests. Shane has developed a concept and a truck that is not only doing things right on the culinary level but also as a successful, moneymaking business. Shane Autrey and Smoke Et Al are really the standard. And while it seems like now that the truck is successful, he could sit back and enjoy things, he doesn't. He continues to strive to constantly grow and improve. He refuses to be complacent, and I admire that so much.

I can't wait to see Smoke Et Al continue to be one of the dominating food trucks on our streets, and I cannot wait to see it grow.

To keep up with Shane and the Smoke Et Al crew and to book your private event, wedding or catering, visit the website (www.smokeetal.com), Facebook page or Twitter feed (@SmokeEtAl).

Smoke Et Al's Guaca'roni Salad
(Recipe provided by Shane Autrey)

2 cups dry macaroni noodles (4 cups cooked)
2 ripe avocados
1 lime, zest reserved, juiced
3 cloves smoked garlic confit (substitute roasted garlic if desired)
¼ cup roasted red pepper
2 tablespoon smoked cider vinegar
3 tablespoons EVOO
1 teaspoon coriander
¼ cup cold water

¼ cup fresh cilantro, chopped
½ cup fresh chives, finely chopped
Salt and pepper to taste

Cook macaroni noodles until al dente and reserve. Peel and pit avocados, smash with the lime juice and zest until smooth. Combine garlic (chopped), red pepper, vinegar, EVOO and coriander, and whisk together. Add cold water as needed to emulsify as a vinaigrette

Fold together avocado and vinaigrette, combine with macaroni noodles and mix in cilantro and chives. The consistency should be smooth and creamy; adjust as needed with additional cold water. Salt and pepper to taste. Keep refrigerated or serve immediately. This is awesome topped with herbed crouton crumbs.

SUM YUM YUM

Born and raised in Laos, Kong was the oldest sibling in his family, so he had to learn to cook at a very young age. He had no choice, so cooking became second nature to him. From his time in Laos to his time now, family has been first and foremost a top priority for Kong. You can very often find his sons, Anthony and Zac, or his wife, Tricia, greeting the customers and taking orders. It is very much a family affair.

Because he has been cooking basically his entire life, he would always cook for everyone—friends, family, co-workers. And everyone always told Kong he should open a restaurant. Unfortunately, the cost of opening a restaurant was just too prohibitive; that is, until one day a friend from Massachusetts mentioned something about a food truck. Kong began to research finding the right concept. Tricia and Kong thought back to their trips to Chinatown in Boston and remembered the bánh mìs they would get there. They had the idea of Americanizing the bánh mì and bringing it to Nashville. They could pair that with Laotian Egg Rolls, as a nod to Kong's heritage. As for the name, Sum Yum Yum, the story is that they liked the phrasing "nom nom." And so they were trying to find something that had the same feel to it. Thus, Sum Yum Yum was born.

I credit Kong for introducing me to the bánh mì. The first day we saw Sum Yum Yum out, Jim and I ordered one of each kind Kong had on the menu, except for the fried tofu. So we received our three bánh mì sandwiches: pork, lemongrass chicken and shredded beef. We enjoyed them all. The pork was our favorite, though. And we absolutely were in love with the egg rolls (which, by the way, won third place in the Best Deep Fried category at the 2013 Nashville Street Food Awards). After we had finished, Kong walked over to where we were sitting to see what we thought of the sandwiches. We gave him our feedback: "They were very tasty. And a good bit spicy!" Jim asked him which was his favorite. Kong said the fried tofu. Jim and I gave each other a look that said, "OK, we have room to try one more sandwich." I really wasn't sure about tofu at this point in time (summer of 2012), so I was a little bit nervous. But when Kong brought the Fried Tofu Bánh Mì over and Jim and I took our first bites, it was game over. It is hands down the best bánh mì in Nashville. Now, anytime we visit a place with multiple food trucks and Sum Yum Yum is there, it's the first stop we make. We want to make sure we don't fill up at the other trucks before we get a chance to get the Fried Tofu Bánh Mì. So we split one and make the deal that if we go around and either of us isn't wowed by the other food or we are still hungry when we leave the event, we will split another Fried Tofu Bánh Mì on our way out. It's that good!

Kong also serves French fries on the truck. Now I have a funny story about the spicy fries. I talk about food trucks a lot. I'm always yelling at my co-workers, "Hey, this truck is over here!" or "This food truck is here today!" Well, one day—and it

was even snowing a bit—one of my co-workers actually jumped and said he was going to the truck. That truck was Sum Yum Yum. It was going to be his first-ever experience visiting Kong. I showed up at the truck just as my co-worker received his order. When I got back to the office, I asked him what he thought. He said, "Man, this sandwich is really, really good. But these spicy fries. They are *so spicy*!" I had never had the fries before, so I just figured "spicy" meant Cajun-seasoned fries, like at Hoss' Loaded Burgers or at some of the local restaurants. But no. These fries were actually spicy. So if you are a fan of spicy, you will appreciate these fries. They are unlike any other spicy fry I have ever had—it's kind of like Nashville Hot Chicken spicy.

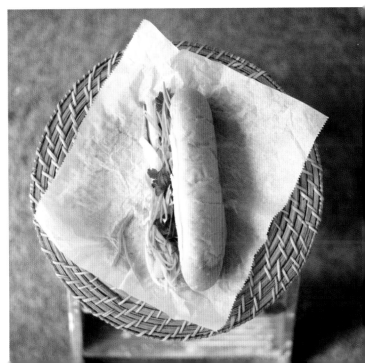

The Laotian Egg Rolls are truly one of the standouts on the truck. They are obviously one of the most popular items, given that an egg roll is so familiar to everyone. They are definitely good sized, and you get two for three dollars. It's not a bad price at all, especially since these are made-from-scratch egg rolls. They are fried to order and perfectly prepared.

Kong and Tricia are truly genuine people. They love seeing and hearing feedback from customers. They love when events go well and they get the opportunity to make a lot of people's bellies happy. They love getting to relax at the end of a night with other food truck owners. And they love when their whole family gets to be

on the truck to greet and help serve customers. These people have such huge hearts. While I am a fan of Kong's bánh mì, this is one of those examples where the personal connection to those on the truck enhances my experience when I visit it. And I think this is something restaurant owners miss out on.

Kong and Tricia are currently focusing on their catering requests. To follow the truck or to book a private event or catering, visit their website (www.sumyumyum. com), Facebook page or Twitter feed (@sum_yum_yum).

TWO GUYS IN A LUNCHBOX

One of my first experiences working with Jeremy Rakestraw and Kris McGee from Two Guys In A Lunchbox was when Jim was organizing food trucks for a Nashville Pittie event. We thought that we would bring our two main loves together: pit-bull awareness and food trucks. A best-of-both-worlds situation. Jeremy and Kris jumped at the chance to serve at the event, especially being dog lovers and pit-bull owners themselves. It was the first time I had ever been able to try their food. At the time, they were doing a loaded French fry concept that they call Twisted Meals. I was pleasantly surprised to see they had a vegetarian wrap on the menu, and it was actually very good.

Having met at work and become friends, they brought years of experience in the food service industry together to create Two Guys In A Lunchbox. Kris has worked in the food industry in every position from dishwasher to private catering chef. Jeremy has a very similar story, having spent his time in professional kitchens from the major chains to the local restaurants. Kris was inspired by Julia Child and has been experimenting in the kitchen nearly his whole life. He can trace his love of food back to when he was ten

years old and was cooking spaghetti pie with his mother. The process—so simple and yet so precise—created flavors that immediately instilled in him a love of huge flavor.

Kris's wife's family bakery back in Maine was the inspiration behind their expansion into the artisan cheese breads they now use on the truck to make all of their sandwiches, like the Nashvillian, which uses a bacon cheese bread. If you are in and around Nashville and can get to the Two Guys truck, you can buy a loaf to take home. It will make following the Nashvillian recipe (included here) a little easier.

When they first started in 2012, they were primarily serving Twisted Meals. Depending on the event, the Twisted Meals do still pop up on the menu. Twisted Meals are a loaded French fry concept topped with things like a mound of bacon and cheese, garlic and parmesan or smoked meats and barbecue sauce. They had some very creative ideas.

In 2013, they reinvented their menu utilizing the artisan breads that they make from scratch. Several gourmet sandwiches like the Nashvillian now populate their menu, along with their Terrible Tacos, which took third place in the Best Taco category at the 2013 Nashville Street Food Awards.

They have expanded to two trucks (they have a sweet truck as well) and are in talks to grow into a brick and mortar. They are just two guys. In a mobile trailer. Making the dream come true.

To keep up with the truck or to book it for a private event or catering, you can check out the website (www.ntmci.com), Facebook page (Two-Guys-In-A-Lunchbox) or Twitter feed (@twoguyslunchbox).

Two Guys In A Lunchbox the Nashvillian (recipe provided by Jeremy Rakestraw)

4 slices thick-cut bacon
2 large eggs
2 teaspoons water
Pinch of salt and pepper
1 medium green tomato
2 cups seasoned breadcrumbs
2 cups canola or vegetable oil
4 slices bacon cheese bread
2 slices cheddar cheese

Start by cooking the bacon (to your liking). Whisk the eggs together with the water, salt and pepper. Set aside. Cut the green tomato into 4 slices about 1-inch thick and dip each slice first into the egg mixture and then into the breadcrumbs.

After heating the oil in a large frying pan to 350 degrees, place the coated tomatoes into the oil for about 3 minutes or until golden brown. Remove the tomatoes from the frying pan and dry the excess oil.

Lay 2 slices of the bacon cheese bread and place a slice of cheddar cheese on each slice. Cut the bacon in half and place half the bacon on top of each slice of cheese. Once the excess oil has been removed from the tomatoes, place 2 slices on each sandwich. Top each with the other slices of bacon cheese bread.

After all ingredients have been placed on the bread, heat a medium-sized skillet at medium temperature. Cook the sandwich for about 2 minutes on each side or until golden brown.

Note: The recipe provided did not specify it, but it would probably be a good idea to butter the sides of the bread that will be grilled.

THE WAFFLE BOSS

Ryan Hall and his wife, Danielle, were looking for a change of culinary scenery. Danielle is the daughter of one of Nashville's best pizza makers, Joey from Joey's House of Pizzas. So she has spent all her life surrounded by the food industry. Ryan has been in food service for a huge majority of his life as well, having spent a large amount of time learning from Danielle's dad at Joey's. Danielle and Ryan eventually opened a Spring Hill location of Joey's House of Pizzas, but after a few years, they really wanted a change. Nashville's food truck scene was at the forefront of every future business owner's attention, and Ryan and Danielle were no exception. Deciding to go the route of the mobile kitchen, they settled on a concept on the opposite end of the spectrum from pizzas and Italian food: chicken and waffles.

At this time, in the summer of 2012, shockingly enough, chicken and waffles had not yet taken Nashville by storm. The chicken and waffles craze really blew up in 2013, and the Waffle Boss was one of the reasons that trend became so mainstream.

One of the truly clever things that the Waffle Boss truck has that no other truck has is a display window. On the side of the truck between the order window and the pickup window is a rectangular display window. Ryan cooks up a few of the different waffles and chicken options that are available that day. He plates them and sets them in the display window so that the customer can actually see the food before ordering it. It also is a way to entice people with the look of your food. A Red Velvet Waffle with cream cheese frosting? It's as delicious as it sounds—and looks—and is a customer favorite.

The chicken on the truck ranges from your everyday familiar breaded chicken tender to Ryan's version of hot chicken. (Just a note: Ryan does have sweet notes in his hot chicken seasoning. So if you love hot chicken and just prefer the hot without the sugary undertones, let him know when you order. He will be able to accommodate making it hot and not sweet.)

The chicken tenders are perfectly breaded and fried. They are a favorite of children and adults alike. This is why the chicken and waffles concept is brilliant: It's kids' food when it needs to be. It's a throwback to childhood food when it needs to be. It's a sophisticated adult dinner when it needs to be.

Then there is the versatility of the waffle. While some chain restaurants are trying to make the waffle a bun or a taco shell, so far that has not trickled down to the Waffle Boss. I'm kind of hoping it never does. The waffle at the Waffle Boss gets to be exactly what it is: a waffle. Ryan can flavor it and make it a Gingerbread Waffle or a Red Velvet Waffle or a Birthday Cake Waffle, but it remains, at its core, a waffle. I appreciate that. And he makes great waffle batter. The waffles are always crisp with a little bit of crunch on the outside but soft, spongy and almost cakey inside. Topped with a drizzle of syrup or cream cheese icing—or, dare I say, ice cream—the waffles are boss on this truck.

Recently, Danielle decided to reenter the brick-and-mortar world, and the Waffle Boss now has a sister establishment in the Spring Hill area of Tennessee called Nellie's. This is not a chicken and waffles joint, but what the opening of Nellie's did do was expand the capabilities of the Waffle Boss with a full commercial kitchen at its disposal instead of a shared commissary space. I'm not knocking the commissary space, but there is a difference when you're working in your own space. It allows Ryan to do more preparation so he can offer more options on the truck. So while Danielle will no longer be on the truck, Ryan is very excited to show you what he can do with the waffle.

To keep up with the Waffle Boss or to book it for your event, you visit its Facebook page or Twitter feed (@WaffleBoss).

The Waffle Boss's Gingerbread Waffles
(Recipe provided by Danielle Hall)

Makes about 4 waffles

3 cups all-purpose flour
4 teaspoons baking powder
2 teaspoons ground cinnamon
2 teaspoons ground ginger
½ teaspoon freshly grated nutmeg (eyeball it)
½ teaspoon salt
4 large eggs
²/₃ cup packed dark brown sugar
1 cup canned pumpkin purée
1¼ cups milk
½ cup molasses
½ cup (1 stick) melted butter, plus some to butter the waffle iron

Mix flour, baking powder, cinnamon, ginger, nutmeg and salt in a bowl. Set aside. In another bowl, beat eggs and brown sugar until fluffy. Mix in pumpkin, milk, molasses and melted butter. Then begin to mix the wet ingredients with the dry ingredients until just absorbed. Be careful not to over mix; lumpy batter is OK.

Brush the waffle iron with butter. Batter is enough to make about 4 waffles. So based on your waffle iron, pour the appropriate amount of batter so that you can make about 4 waffles.

Yayo's OMG

Yayo's OMG has taken the Nashville food truck scene by storm. It is one of the most popular trucks, amassing long lines everywhere it goes. In fact, Nashville mayor Karl Dean visited the truck during the filming of its *Eat Street* episode on the Cooking Channel.

Yayo's OMG is a true family affair. Chef Yayo, his wife and their daughter work side by side each and every day on the truck. His wife and daughter are, of course, his top taste testers as well. Chef Yayo (Yayo is actually a nickname) Jimenez grew up in Cuautla, Mexico, which is the third-largest city in the Morelos state of Mexico. Morelos has a storied history and culture and is home to delicious culinary creations. Yayo's love of food dates back to the earliest memories of his childhood, when his grandmother Chechis had a home full of good food and mouth-watering aromas. She shared with Yayo the joy she had for food and cooking, and he treasures those memories to this day. They are what inspire, him and he credits Chechis with instilling in him the philosophy that "in food and in life, quality is always more important than quantity." That philosophy definitely comes through when you taste his creations.

Family means everything to Chef Yayo. When his wife and daughters moved to Nashville so that his eldest daughter, Giovy, could pursue her dream in music as a singer/songwriter, he followed them to Nashville (from Miami) as soon as he could. The food truck scene was just starting to grow here, so after much discussion, the family came to the decision to spread their love of gourmet Mexican food to Tennessee utilizing the food truck concept. As they were thinking of names, they settled on the childhood nickname Yayo and a play on words—well, letters, really. "OMG," which officially stands for "Original Gourmet Mexican," could also stand for "Oh. My. Goodness!" I say that whenever I get a chance to eat Yayo's mahi-mahi tacos!

When you walk up to the truck, you are greeted by either Chef Yayo's wife, Ingrid, or his daughter Giovy. Ingrid is such a fireball, she brings a smile to my face every time I see her at the window. I can only imagine that she keeps Chef Yayo on his toes. Even with her hair pulled back and a cap on, Giovy brightens the truck with her unassuming beauty and warm smile. And while she isn't as much of a fireball as her mother, she still brings so much personality to the truck. The experience you get when you visit them at the window is unlike anywhere else. Even times when I don't eat from their truck, I always have to stop and visit with them. I enjoy talking with them, and I always leave with a bellyache from laughing so hard and aching cheeks from smiling so much. I should mention that normally they are so busy that I

don't get to enter into any lengthy dialogue with them, and I don't mind that at all. Keep them busy, Nashville!

As I was just starting to get into food trucks back in 2012, I remember I kept hearing things about Yayo's OMG and its mahi-mahi tacos. I thought to myself, "Could they be *that* great?" I mean, when people would talk food trucks, they would mention the Grilled Cheeserie and the mahi-mahi tacos from Yayo's OMG. And yes, folks, they really can be *that* good. While they are super stuffed, so you may need to eat a piece of the mahi-mahi before you can pick up the taco to eat it, the coleslaw has that nice crunch and crispness and just a little bit of tang. You get the cooling creaminess from the cilantro sauce, and then comes the beer-battered mahi-mahi. The nice crunch of the batter and the flavor of the mahi-mahi make it a truly a special taco. It was recently nominated as one of the Top 15 Food Truck Tacos by online industry publication *Mobile Cuisine*.

The Legend Tacos are another of my favorite things from Chef Yayo. They contain a mixture of brisket, chorizo and chicharrón and are then topped with onions and cilantro and either hot or mild salsa. I do love brisket, and the spiciness from the chorizo adds a lot of extra flavor.

THE TRUCKS

What Yayo's calls on its menu the Steak Mexican Melt, you might call a steak quesadilla. Chef Yayo? He calls it a hamburger. I call it delicious! It's one of those familiar items to anyone who has ever gone to a Mexican restaurant. But while it stays true to what a quesadilla is, the steak is grilled perfectly, having just a little bit of char and crunch. The cheese is melted, gooey and creamy. The browned and grilled tortilla is perfectly crisp. All of it melts together to be better than any quesadilla from those Mexican restaurants you think make great quesadillas. I always get the sour cream on the top because I like having an off bite where you get that cool, creamy mixture with the melted creamy cheese. It's a perfect option for those days when you want something gourmet but still want simple and familiar.

Yayo's is always running weekly specials. From its Chalupitas, which were featured on *Eat Street*, to their Pambazos to the traditional Torta, you never know what will inspire Chef Yayo's special each week. I don't get to try their specials as much as I would like because I can't always get to their truck every week. After seeing the Chalupitas, I was really dying to try them. They are pretty labor-intensive to make, so they don't make it to the weekly specialty menu as often. So finally, after harassing Chef Yayo almost weekly, they made it back on the menu for a one-week-only limited engagement. I tweeted ahead that Jim and I were coming, and I'm glad I did because sweet Giovy kept count of how many Chalupitas shells were left on the truck to ensure that they wouldn't sell out before we got there. (Sometimes having friends inside the truck is a benefit. What am I saying…it's always a benefit!) To make these tasty items, a cornmeal cup that almost tastes like a cornbread cake doughnut is filled with refried beans, slow-roasted pork and mashed potatoes and then topped and garnished with cheese, sour cream, cilantro and onions. They were a lot bigger than I thought they would be. It was good that Jim and I were splitting an order because I almost couldn't finish one, and there are two in an order.

Chef Yayo has been cooking nearly his entire life, but he still has a desire to continue learning more and more about his art. And as he continues, we continue to get better and better OMG eats.

I mention several times throughout this book how humble the food truck owners are, and Chef Yayo, Ingrid and Giovy are no exception. When I asked Chef Yayo about his favorite moments on the truck and some of the highlights of being a food truck owner, his response was that every day was a highlight. Every day was his favorite moment. Every time they open the window, they are still humbled that people choose to come eat their food, talk about their food on social media and come back again and again. They still revel in the excitement of seeing new faces and witnessing customers' reactions to their food. The patronage at the truck inspires Yayo to continue cooking and to continue to grow. The more we love his food, the more it confirms to him that he chose the right path and is doing the right thing. He says, "We can't forget that it's the customers who make our business what it is, and we truly appreciate their support."

The future for Yayo's OMG is bright. Yayo and his family just want to continue to focus on what they do well: making great "Original Mexican Gourmet" by paying attention to detail so they can give Nashvillians a "rich culinary experience."

To keep up with Yayo's OMG or book it for a private event or catering, visit the truck's website (www.yayosomg.com), Facebook page (Yayo's O.M.G.) or Twitter feed (@yayosomg).

Yayo's OMG Mahi-Mahi Fish Tacos
(Recipe provided by Chef Yayo Jimenez)

Recipe time: 25 minutes / Yields 1 serving (2 tacos)

Mahi-Mahi:
8 ounces mahi-mahi fillets, cut into even strips
¾ cup dark beer
1 cup vegetable oil, for frying
1 cup all-purpose flour
1 teaspoon paprika
1 teaspoon cayenne pepper
1 teaspoon salt

Marinate the mahi-mahi strips in the beer for 5 to 7 minutes. Heat the oil over medium heat until hot. Mix together the flour, paprika, cayenne and salt in a large bowl and then dredge the mahi-mahi strips, one at a time, in the flour mixture. Lightly fry the fish until golden brown (about 90 seconds to 2 minutes).

Coleslaw:
6 tablespoons red cabbage, cut into tiny pieces
6 tablespoons white cabbage, cut into tiny pieces
6 tablespoons carrots, shredded
10 tablespoons orange juice
Salt and freshly ground pepper

Combine the cabbages with the carrots and then mix in the orange juice. Season with salt and pepper.

Cilantro Sauce:
10 tablespoons sour cream
6 tablespoons fresh cilantro
2 small cloves garlic
2 tablespoons freshly squeezed lemon juice
Salt and freshly ground pepper

Blend together the sour cream, cilantro, garlic and lemon juice in a blender. Season with salt and pepper.

Assemble:
4 4-inch corn tortillas for serving
Oil for heating tortillas

Heat the tortillas in a skillet with a little bit of oil. Layer 2 tortillas per taco. Add coleslaw and top with mahi-mahi strips followed by some more coleslaw. Finish off with cilantro sauce.

Bao Down

Tristan Chiu is probably one of the most well put together yet casually dressed people I have ever met. He's also a pescatarian, and I had him meet me at Martin's Bar-B-Que. Yeah, I'm the girl who brought a pescatarian to a barbecue joint. Tristan is quick to point out that they did have catfish, and it was delicious!

Tristan moved to Nashville about three years ago to help open a certain major department store in the Green Hills area of town as a personal stylist. After moving on from the department store late in 2013, Tristan went home for the holidays to Chicago, where his childhood friend Eric Tran was also home for the holidays. Eric Tran moved from Chicago to New York to go to culinary school and pursue the culinary arts. He had come home for the holidays to surprise his family before he left to cook and spend some time in Shanghai. While both Eric and Tristan were home, they began to talk about what would be the next step in their lives, and the idea of a food truck popped up. While Chicago is their home, it is a very expensive place to get mobile vendors licenses and permits, and the city is also oversaturated with food trucks and mobile vendors. It's the same in New York City. Having witnessed the boom in the food truck scene in Nashville, Tristan suggested bringing their truck concept here to our streets.

Since that time, they have secured their concept, their brand and a mini school bus; launched an indiegogo campaign; and set up a pop-up dinner to introduce Nashville to Bao Down.

Tristan makes the point that when it comes to their baos, it is important to him that they are done right and that the ingredients are the freshest available. He doesn't want to serve something that he wouldn't be proud to eat himself, and having healthy ingredients that are good for you and your body is a top priority. Their bao dough is dairy free (lactose intolerant folks put your hands up!). They are partnering with local farms to source their ingredients as much as possible. They want to create foods from unprocessed ingredients.

According to Tristan, they make a traditional Chinese bao where the filling is wrapped inside the bao like a dumpling. This is not the Taiwanese-style bao that is open faced, similar to a taco. If you are a bao person, you know what I'm talking about. If you are not a bao person, when you visit Bao Down, you will immediately understand what I'm talking about. They want their baos to be authentic and fun and still appeal to the Nashville market. So there will be a plethora of options for the vegetarian and the meat loving alike, with flavors from the mainstream to authentic flavors that will blow your mind.

They created an indiegogo fundraising campaign not only to help get their business running but also as a way to get Nashville consumers more excited about their concept and get them involved and feel like part of the process. It is a brilliant strategy when done right. Please note: fundraising campaigns *will not* work for everyone. I am not suggesting that all new trucks should fundraise in this manner, but for Tristan and Eric, thanks to their personalities and the vibe of Bao Down, this concept fits what they are trying to do.

Also in the spring of 2014, they have planned a few pop-up dinners at their friend's restaurant Kohana in Green Hills. You can get a taste of what the truck will offer and meet the brains behind the baos.

Tristan was also kind enough to bring me some sample mushroom baos. In the last few years, I have really come to enjoy mushrooms. And the mushrooms in this bao and the bao dough worked really well. The mushrooms were covered in sauce that was full of Asian flavor and spices, and the bao dough was perfectly soft and spongy. I could probably eat about a dozen of these—they were flavorful without feeling heavy. I can't wait to try some of their meat-loving baos.

Hoping to open early in the summer of 2014, Tristan and Eric say they have some fun plans set up for customers who are waiting in line. Tristan would not divulge what that was but did say, "Our customers are going to have fun when they get in our line." They don't want Bao Down to be just a great food truck; they want you to have so much fun that it is more of an experience.

They have also adopted the goal of reinvesting in the community, especially to help fight hunger. Tristan got very serious when he spoke about this because, he said, being part of a community goes both ways. You not only get to give people great food and enjoy running your business, but you also need to make sure that you are contributing to making that community even better. As the community strives, it allows your business to strive. It is really great to see so many trucks beginning to adopt this same philosophy. Tristan hopes that Bao Down will really be on the forefront of this movement among food trucks.

To keep up with the progress of Bao Down, you can visit its website (www. baodownnashville.com), Facebook page and Twitter feed (@baodownTN).

Bao Down's Braised Short Rib
(Recipe provided by Tristan Chiu)

2 pounds short rib (can be bone in or out)
2 garlic cloves, halved
1 medium-sized onion, largely diced
2 ounces ginger, sliced
1 bunch scallions, sliced
1 large carrot, largely diced
2 stalks celery, largely diced
1 jalapeño, cut in fourths
4 star anise
4 cloves
1 cinnamon stick
1 teaspoon coriander
1 cup soy sauce (you can also use chicken stock or wine)

Lightly season the short rib with salt and pepper. In a large saucepot, sear on medium heat until the meat is caramelized on all 4 sides. Take the short rib out and set aside.

Add the veggies and spices to the pot and sweat the veggies until they start to soften and the spices become aromatic.

Place the short rib back in the pot and add all the liquid (soy sauce, wine or stock). The liquid should just barely cover the meat.

Cover the pot with a lid or aluminum foil and place in an oven heated to 250 degrees for 2½ to 3 hours.

You should be able to poke the meat with ease. Remove the meat and set aside. Strain the liquid and reserve to use in cooking for a later meal as stock.

BARE NAKED BAGEL

College friends Justin Buttner and Robert Kane are bringing something to Nashville that is highly anticipated by many in the food community: the New York–style bagel. Now before I go any further, both Justin and Robert are upstate New York natives. Justin lists Collegetown Bagels as the bagel place he grew up loving and says it's what fed his desire to start his own bagel business. He and his wife have lived here in Nashville for about three years and have absolutely fallen in love with middle Tennessee. But there was just one minor problem: Justin couldn't find a good New York–style bagel anywhere in town. He found good bagels around town, but when you want a New York–style bagel, you want a New York–style bagel. You accept no substitutes. After spending his last few years in the corporate sales world and really craving that bagel, Justin decided maybe it was time for a change.

Robert has spent the majority of his life in a commercial kitchen. Starting as a busboy/dishwasher and then moving on to work for a small upscale catering company for the last ten years, he felt it was time to make a change from the catering. Connecting with Justin, they discussed the possibilities of becoming business partners. Robert moved down here to Nashville, and Bare Naked Bagel was born.

Having bought the trailer formerly owned by Loco Donuts, Justin and Robert started building the brand and the business. Justin is handling the business side of things, while Robert will be handling the culinary side. They've chosen the name Bare Naked Bagel because, first off, it rolls off the tongue pretty easily. But more importantly, Robert's passion is food. And he really is going to do as much as he can possibly do from scratch, utilizing unprocessed ingredients. So the Bare Naked name also is a representation of their philosophy of using ingredients in their bare-naked form. They are partnering with many local farms so that they know the farmers where their ingredients come from. They know and understand the processes that their meats, cheeses, fruits, vegetables and grains go through. One of the steps you have to take in making a great product is knowing about your ingredients.

I can't tell you how excited I was to hear this. Not only were they bringing a brilliant concept to Nashville, but also they were going to do it right. They are making their own cream cheeses. They are making their own relishes and fruit chutneys and jams. And while they obviously have bagels, they will be creating bagel sandwiches as well. The bagel is very versatile, working well in everything from breakfast to burgers to sandwiches. And Justin and Robert can't wait to explore all the possibilities and introduce you to the bagel in its simplest form and to its gourmet sibling.

I was lucky enough to be gifted with a few sample bagels—a plain bagel, an everything bagel, a cinnamon raisin bagel and their Bacon Bleu bagel. These bagels were really delicious! I was sad when I ran out of samples, and now I'm waiting for the truck to have its grand opening so I can fill up by bagel basket. (I don't currently have a bagel basket, but I'm going to have one!) The Bacon Bleu was really the standout for me. They put the bacon and the bleu cheese inside the bagel—it is baked *into* the bagel. All it was missing was a folded omelet in between.

The thing that Justin points out will differentiate their bagels is the process. Too many bagel makers are rushing through the process of bagel making so they can make lots of bagels to fill their shelves. Justin and Robert are going to take their time making the dough and properly proofing the dough. It's a one- to two-day process to make the bagels. They can't just go to the store in the morning, make the bagel dough and have it ready to serve to you at lunch. They have to begin prepping a day or two in advance. And for those who have heard that New York bagels are New York bagels because of the minerals and the makeup of the water, when I asked Justin and Robert about this, all they would say is that they are aware of this theory and do have a few secrets when it comes to the water used in making their bagels.

Even though they are transplants to Nashville and middle Tennessee, Justin and Robert have fallen head over heels for this community. It is important to them for Bare Naked Bagel to have a philanthropic focus and reinvest in the community. And they are partnering with several local nonprofit organizations to do just that.

There are a lot of trucks that enter the food truck scene each year. And there are always a few standouts. Bare Naked Bagels is setting itself up to be at the top of this year's New Truck Class of 2014. It is set to open in the early spring of 2014. It is already on a rotation to be at a few of the local farmers' markets throughout the summer (one of which is only miles from my house so I could not be more excited!).

Let's welcome Justin and Robert to the food truck scene and to our city. Run, don't walk, to their window.

To follow their progress, keep up with the truck or to start booking your private event, visit their website (www.barenakedbagel.com), Facebook page or Twitter feed (@barenakedbagel).

Bare Naked Bagel's Cranberry Relish
(Recipe provided by Robert Kane)

1 cup water
½ cup orange juice
1 cup sugar
12 ounces fresh cranberries
6 ounces mandarin oranges, drained

Combine water, orange juice, sugar and cranberries in a medium saucepan. Bring to a boil and reduce to medium heat. Simmer for 10 to 12 minutes, stirring occasionally. The cranberries will start to burst, and the mixture should thicken slightly. Remove from heat and stir in the mandarin oranges. Cover and let cool completely at room temperature. Refrigerate for up to one week.

Suggestions for use:
Use in a Bare Naked Bagel "Thanksgiving Left-Over" signature sandwich (a bagel sandwich with roasted, sliced turkey breast and homemade stuffing topped with cranberry relish) or swirl into cream cheese and top your favorite bagel for a sweet snack.

FINAL THOUGHTS

With new trucks popping up nearly every week here in Nashville, and with trucks moving from other cities like Austin, I am looking forward to seeing how the scene changes and adapts.

To the food truck owner: I hope that you will not only hold yourself to a high standard but also hold your fellow food truck owners to the same. Unlike a brick-and-mortar restaurant, your business is affected by the experiences people have at other food trucks. The food you put out your window affects how people look at food trucks. Even if your food truck is making amazing food, like the trucks featured in this book are doing, people will pass you over without giving your gourmet eats a try if they have had a bad experience at another truck. Remember as a child when you learned the word "dog" but you called everything on four legs a dog? The cow, the cat, the giraffe—they were all dogs to your childhood self. It's the same mindset. After one bad food truck experience, people will look at your food truck business as if it is the same. So hold your comrades accountable for their quality and service. It takes just one bad apple to spoil the barrel, particularly when it comes to issues and regulations imposed by the government.

Pricing will always be a debate in this town. Most people are going to get antsy when they see anything on a food truck menu board priced at ten dollars or more (before sides, chips or drinks), regardless of whether they would pay that in a heartbeat at a lesser-quality brick and mortar. You need to make us, the consumers, understand why we should pay what you are charging. Sometimes you might need to explain with more than just the words "craft" or "locally sourced" ingredients. Those are starting to become buzzwords that people shrug off—they're being thrown around so much that they're losing their potency. Hoss' Loaded Burgers has a burger called the Italian Job, and it is typically about one dollar more than its other burgers. Hoss explains that the burger patty is a mix of his grass-fed beef and a higher-cost sausage from Porter

Road Butcher. The cost to create the burger went up by one dollar per burger. Delta Bound mentions that there are items on its menu that it could price higher. But when the owners look at profit margins, they keep the price down maybe one or two dollars more than what it should be to keep it under that ten-dollar mark, then they pair these items with others that can make up for the lower profit margin. This way, they can still hit their price points and income goals while at the same time offer some higher-quality menu items, even if the profit margin on those items is a little lower than they'd like. It's not always about what you think you deserve to make on that product. Every consumer has a price limit in his or her head and will not spend over that amount. So while I personally don't mind spending a little more at the food trucks because I understand what goes into everything, the general public doesn't always have that same knowledge, and a lot of times, they don't care to. They want good food at a reasonable price. And if it comes to them on a food truck—bonus points.

It is also important to consider the location in which you are serving. If you are at a business park, perhaps consider putting a five-dollar item on your menu that day for the employee on a budget. Find a way to appeal to the customers to get them to your truck—because odds are, if you get them to your truck and they like your food, the next time they visit your truck, they'll purchase a more expensive entrée or sandwich. Build that repeat business. Additionally, if they are with a group and everything is more than what they can spend, they'll take their entire lunch group elsewhere, regardless of whether the other members don't mind the prices. People on budgets and people on health kicks will dominate where a group eats lunch no matter how big the group.

To the consumer: Expand what you think you know about food trucks. Expand what you think you know about food. Expand what you are willing to try. I've had pickles twice this year in less than three months after having gone probably thirty years without eating a pickle. It might seem minor, but I allowed a food truck to expand what I was willing to try, and I tried it again because I liked it. If you don't know how to pronounce something, don't automatically cross that off of your list. Ask the person at the window. You might just be talking to the chef! And chefs love talking about their food and explaining their menu items. Some of the interviews for this book lasted two hours, and we weren't even ready to stop talking. Don't know what a bánh mì is? Never had foie gras? Allow the trucks to introduce you to new things. The owners can talk you through it, and sometimes you might be able to get a sample before buying the full item. Dallas from Hoss' Loaded Burgers gave me a sample of his Umami Ketchup before I tried the burger since traditionally I'm not a ketchup fan and he knew that. But I liked the sample of the Umami Ketchup, and I'm glad he offered it to me. I guess all this is to say: don't be afraid.

I will also add that if you have a bad experience with a food truck, *do not* judge the rest of the food truck community on that experience or compare it to that truck.

FINAL THOUGHTS

I've had some pretty bad experiences at food trucks, but I've had even more amazing experiences at food trucks. I would have missed some of the most amazing food I've ever had if I had stopped going to the food trucks after the first bad experience. Does every food truck hit every menu item out of the park? No. I don't even hold that against the food truck. If it's a new truck that I've never tried before, I'll go back a second time and try something different. My philosophy is normally three tries and you're out. Yes, there are a few trucks that I tried only once before they were permanently benched. In order to make my banned list, the entire experience has to be ridiculously bad. So again, I can't reiterate it enough: do not hold the entire community of food trucks responsible for a bad experience with a truck.

The new generation of food trucks is not the roach coaches people think. Yayo's OMG is by far the best example of how much trucks are *not* roach coaches. If Yayo isn't busy, I dare you to ask if he'll open the door for you to look in the kitchen—not to go in but to see just how clean it is inside that truck. And Chef Yayo isn't the only one running a tight ship when it comes to cleanliness. I'm only using him as an example because I've actually seen his pristine kitchen with my own two eyes. I can see the clean of a truck when I walk up and glance at the inside. These are health department–regulated professional kitchens.

Don't be fair-weather food truck fans! With the creation of ToGoOrder.com and a majority of the trucks utilizing this service (when it fits their business models), you can use the ToGoOrder website or application or the NFTA application on your Smartphone to preorder, prepay and even pick what time you'd like to pick up the order. No waiting in line. No waiting for food to be prepared. You stay in your air-conditioned office or your heated home until it's time to walk outside to grab your order. You spend mere moments outside in the elements. And since you've prepaid, you don't even need to carry anything with you. If a truck is not utilizing this service, it's because it doesn't apply to its model or perhaps it is serving at a special event like a beer festival.

Finally, food trucks should not be compared to fast food. The food concept is completely different. The food truck is a restaurant that is mobile. Be patient and wait a few extra minutes. Because we aren't sitting at a restaurant, obviously the food truck owners know they have to prepare everything more quickly, but the majority make your food when you order it (unlike fast food, which is pre-prepared). It will take a minute or two more. And it will be worth the wait, I promise.

I want to end this book with one more thought, and it is the way I end most of my blog posts. When you go to a truck, try something new. And most importantly, I'll see you all at the trucks!

Julie Festa is Nashville's premier food truck blogger, having created and run NashvilleFoodTruckJunkie.com since 2012. She keeps up with the trucks' locations and reviews them to help middle Tennesseans enjoy the best possible food truck experience. From organizing food truck schedules on the blog to scheduling trucks to serve on the corporate properties she helps to manage or inviting trucks to participate in local animal awareness/activist events such as Nashville's Pittie Fest, Julie has incorporated her love of food trucks into every aspect of her life. She also is a huge hockey fan and sponsors a local hockey podcast to help get hockey fans to the food trucks pre- and post games. Having lived in Nashville for a third of her life, Julie absolutely loves the city and wants to share all that it has to offer, especially the mobile food culture.

Visit us at
www.historypress.net

———————•———————

This title is also available as an e-book.